To Tenny, Dorothy, and Ellen Swilley

Mobile Commerce

Mobile Commerce

How It Contrasts, Challenges and Enhances Electronic Commerce

Esther Swilley

BUSINESS EXPERT PRESS

Mobile Commerce: How It Contrasts, Challenges and Enhances Electronic Commerce

Copyright © Business Expert Press, LLC, 2016.

First published in 2016 by
Business Expert Press, LLC
222 East 46th Street, New York, NY 10017
www.businessexpertpress.com

ISBN-13: 978-1-60649-844-6 (paperback)
ISBN-13: 978-1-60649-845-3 (e-book)

Business Expert Press Digital and Social Media Marketing and Advertising Collection

Collection ISSN: 2333-8822 (print)
Collection ISSN: 2333-8830 (electronic)

Cover and interior design by Exeter Premedia Services Private Ltd., Chennai, India

First edition: 2016

10 9 8 7 6 5 4 3 2 1

Printed in the United States of America.

Abstract

Do you know anyone who does *not* own a mobile device? Consumers use mobile devices not only for communicating but for shopping as well. Searching for product information, inquiring about services, comparing prices, and purchasing make up just some of the shopping functions done on mobile devices. How does digital change how firms do business? What are the differences between desktop computer shoppers and mobile device shoppers? Moreover, are firms prepared to do business in this changing environment? As tablet owners relax in the evenings, they are powering up those tablets, and using tablet time for shopping. Does this behavior differ from those sitting at their desktop computers and browse online? Understanding the differences between those shopping in electronic commerce and those purchasing in mobile commerce allows firms to gain a larger foothold in the digital commerce market.

The purpose of this book is to answer questions concerning the benefits of mobile commerce and its commonalities and contrasts with electronic commerce. Electronic commerce is still viable and we examine its validity along with mobile commerce. Mobile commerce is not electronic commerce, and we discuss the differences, as well as how one can enhance the other. Consumers use both electronic commerce and mobile commerce, as well as offline shopping, on their path to purchase in total omnichannel environment—using all channels. We integrate the opportunities and challenges to bring an idea of the future of marketing with an emphasis on both mobile and electronic commerce, into digital commerce.

Keywords

digital commerce, digital shopping experience, electronic commerce, mobile commerce, omnichannel, strategy, touchpoint

Contents

Acknowledgments

I would like to thank Alexandra Boyd and Victoria Crittenden for all of their assistance.

Introduction

Do you know anyone who does *not* own a mobile device? Over 90 percent of consumers in the United States own a mobile phone and 42 percent own a tablet computer (Pew Research Center 2014). Consumers use mobile devices not only for communicating but with businesses as well. Searching for product information, inquiring about services, comparing prices, and purchasing comprise just some of the shopping functions done on mobile devices. How does digital change how firms do business? What are the differences between desktop computer shoppers and mobile device shoppers? Moreover, are firms prepared to do business in this changing environment? As tablet owners relax in the evenings, they are powering up those tablets, and using tablet time for shopping. Does this behavior differ from those sitting at their desktop computers and browse online? Understanding the differences between those shopping in electronic commerce and those purchasing in mobile commerce allows firms to gain a larger foothold in the digital commerce market.

Shopping on a mobile device has a year-over-year growth rate of 24 percent, and represents 10 percent of total digital commerce spending (comScore 2014). The expected rate of mobile commerce growth for the next few years is around 10 percent per year. Year-over-year e-commerce growth is slowing, while m-commerce growth may soon overtake e-commerce (Madrigal 2014).

Mobile devices connect consumer to all types of products and services. In fact, more than 50 percent of Walmart website visits are on mobile devices (Madrigal 2014). Purchases range from small downloads to large luxury goods. Selling services including insurance, bank-related, even stock trading services occurs on mobile devices. Thus, the revenue generated by mobile devices is growing. The average order value, or the revenue generated per order, is growing for both e-commerce and m-commerce.

Second to Black Friday (sometimes overtaking), Cyber Monday, the Monday after Thanksgiving, is the largest online shopping day of the year. More consumers shop online on this day than any other day of the year.

Many of those shoppers are doing so on their mobile devices. In 2014, 22 percent of Cyber Monday sales were from mobile traffic (IBM 2014). The overall average order value for Cyber Monday was $124. For tablet users the average order value was $121.49 and $99.61 for mobile phone users (IBM 2014). Retailers are seeing value in mobile commerce sales. Yet, most businesses are unaware of how to harness the power of mobile commerce for revenue and consumer relationship building.

The consumer's journey along the path to purchase has changed. How consumers move from need to purchase is much more complex. Not only have behaviors changed, noticed as consumers went from offline to online shopping, but also the resources used along the path. Search patterns, devices, recommenders, time, and location changed within the last 10 years. As mobile web traffic increases, taking advantage of these changes eludes many businesses. Retailers are unsure of how to take advantage of mobile in the consumer's path to purchase. Businesses are getting lost, taking the wrong road, and need a roadmap. As businesses waffle, consumers are moving ahead.

Has the path to purchase changed electronic commerce shopping? Yes and no. Is online shopping going away? No way! Firms need to understand how to mesh online and mobile for the good of both the business and the customer. Consumers have not moved away from online shopping. Consumers have included mobile shopping. Businesses must learn to incorporate both.

How mobile is affecting online shopping is the question that businesses want to answer. Convoluted, the path to purchase contains many twists and turns. Shopping may start on a mobile device, online, or in the store and end on mobile, online, or in the store. Firms are still stumbling to synchronize clicks and bricks. However, now mobile is in the mix. Consumers are showing that mobile is shifting how they shop—from one retailer to the next, from one device to the next in one shopping trip, many times in just a few minutes in one location.

Mobile has the ability to transform business. It is bringing more customers, more interactivity, more engagement, and hopefully more revenues. Mobile did not happen with social. Likes did not translate into dollars. However, mobile commerce is not social commerce. Mobile commerce is not electronic commerce. Mobile commerce, however, does give firms the chance to extend other commerce opportunities. Mobile gives businesses the benefits of time and location. No longer do firms have to wait to interact with customers, nor do customers wait to interact with businesses. Mobile allows for interactions that are more individual. Personalization has truly become real.

Now, as with e-commerce, firms want to understand the value of going mobile and realize its potential as a strategic competitive advantage. Mobile commerce (m-commerce) refers to the ability to offer value through virtual transactions that allow for location-specificity and time-sensitivity, as well as the ability to build personalized relationships with the customer. It is not a by-product of e-commerce. There are certainly areas in which m-commerce can give firms an edge over their competition. Its ubiquity in location and time allows for the marketing of products and services to individuals anytime and anywhere. Translation of competencies learned through e-commerce, as well as the relational resources, to an m-commerce platform, can aid firms in gaining a faster and stronger foothold in the m-commerce arena. However, these resources must hold value not only for the firm, but also for the customer as well (Clulow, Barry, and Gerstman 2007). As consumer value is an essential element of competitive advantage (Fahy and Smithee 1999), firms seeking to use m-commerce as a marketing tool must keep in mind the value to the consumer and not the value of the technology, as was the case with many of the dot.com ventures. Many businesses are reluctant to invest in mobile commerce. There are costs involved, yet the benefits reaped by firms can offset the costs. Businesses must be willing to invest in the technology and marketing efforts needed to develop a robust mobile commerce platform that will thrive.

The proliferation of mobile devices has shown that mobile communications is a worldwide cultural phenomenon. Development of mobile commerce came about by users of mobile phones, tablet computers and other handheld devices. From school age children to corporate board members, most consumers have some sort of mobile communication device. Mobile devices are useful for personal communication through audio, video, and data outputs, and pertinent for organizations marketing through entertainment, promotion, customer service, and commerce transactions.

Several advantages exist for consumers, as well as marketers, in using mobile devices for shopping purposes. Marketers can target based on location to those customers within a geographic area. Identification of nearby patrons stimulates location-based promotions. Since most mobile devices have a single owner, personalization, along with location flexibility, allows for anywhere, anytime, transactions. However, there are also a number of disadvantages of m-commerce. Usability issues are of concern, including the smaller screen. In addition, most mobile devices are not as fast as desktop computers, nor do they have the battery life capacity for extended periods. With disadvantages aside, mobile commerce is a viable marketing channel.

Firms must question the value of several online strategies—electronic commerce, social commerce, and mobile commerce. Because of the time and costs of each, firms need to evaluate the value of each of these approaches. One way of assessment is determining the advantages these online strategies give to firms in the marketplace. Firms are more likely to develop a mobile commerce strategy because of the advantage it would give over the competition. Firms that are eager to choose a mobile commerce strategy will find mobile commerce aids in the development relationship with customers through interactivity.

The purpose of this book is to answer questions concerning the benefits of mobile commerce, and its commonalities and contrasts with electronic commerce, for a digital commerce model. We begin with an overview of what mobile commerce really is—a definition as well as an understanding of the devices used for mobile commerce. Looking at the value of mobile commerce to firms, we present practical applications of mobile commerce. How to develop a mobile strategy is key. We discuss how to develop and incorporate mobile commerce with other business strategies for effective mobile marketing.

Electronic commerce is still viable and we examine its validity along with mobile commerce. Mobile commerce is not electronic commerce, and we discuss the differences, as well as how one can enhance the other. Consumers use both electronic commerce and mobile commerce, as well as offline shopping, on the path to purchase, and using all in combination effectively can enrich the shopping experience. Lastly, we discuss total omnichannel marketing—using all channels effectively. We integrate the opportunities and challenges to bring an idea of the future of marketing, with an emphasis on both mobile and electronic commerce.

As early as 2002, Zhang and Yuan (2002) identified three dimensions of differences between mobile commerce and electronic commerce—technology, business models, and services rendered. We expand on these dimensions to discuss the devices used (technology), strategy and business model differences, and differences in retail services in an omnichannel environment.

Bringing practical information and ideas to both businesses, students of business, as well as those who are truly interested in mobile is the value of this book. It should be of benefit to those wanting to understand one of the routes in the path to purchase.

CHAPTER 1

What Is Digital Commerce?

Electronic commerce and mobile commerce are a part of digital commerce overall. Digital commerce refers to transactions that occur through the Internet. Digital commerce transactions usually begin with the consumer connected online through electronic means. Electronic devices include desktop computers, laptops, mobile phones, and tablets. Digital commerce forms include electronic commerce, mobile commerce, and social commerce. The division of forms is either by device or by platform.

Electronic commerce is any form of economic activity conducted via electronic connections (Wigand 1997). Although this definition is very broad, it has narrowed as digital commerce has advanced. Electronic commerce concerns transactions take place on a desktop computer or laptop, mobile commerce transactions take place on a mobile phone or tablet, and social commerce is on social platform—with some overlap as electronic or mobile devices can conduct social commerce.

What Is Mobile Commerce?

When developed first, electronic commerce on a mobile device defined mobile commerce. Those who were heavily involved with e-commerce were the first adopters of transactions on their mobile devices (Einav et al. 2014) and defined mobile commerce activities in this vein. However, as digital commerce evolved, so did mobile commerce. Mobile commerce came into its own as a viable means of shopping. Mobile commerce is not a form of electronic commerce but a different marketing channel based on changes in consumer behavior and needs.

Mobile commerce, specifically, refers to the ability to offer value through virtual transactions that allow for location-specificity and time-sensitivity, as well as the ability to build personalized relationships with the customer (Swilley and Hofacker 2006). Whereas electronic commerce only offers, the ability to transact at any time, mobile commerce offers consumers the ability to transact at any place and at any time.

Why Mobile Commerce Matters?

Projections of mobile commerce for shopping will increase year over year according to many sources. Although consumers still shop in stores and on their computers, there are reasons for continuance of mobile commerce by consumers. First, anytime, anywhere shopping matters to consumers. Consumers expect to be able to connect to their mobile devices at any location. With their device in hand, use of mobile devices for searching and shopping, anywhere at any time is a marketing function that consumers expect from retailers. Mobile commerce has benefits not found in other forms of shopping, whether online or offline, which include

- Ubiquity
- Location
- High level of ownership
- Individual devices

Ubiquity. Mobile commerce is ubiquitous, meaning consumers shop anywhere at any time. In electronic commerce, using a desktop computer does not allow shopping anyway. Desktop computers are stationary. Consumers must shop at the location of the computer, when online at that computer. Laptops allow for better location advantages but can be cumbersome in trying to shop in many settings. Although the location is not fixed, laptops are usually limited in where usage can take place as many use a laptop instead of a desktop. Hence, the base of the purchase is the whereabouts of the computer.

With electronic commerce, the time it takes to get back to the location of the computer delays the time between when the consumer makes the decision to purchase and the time of purchase. Many factors change that decision within that time. In addition, consumers can shop at locations outside the retail store, including while at a sporting event, on public transportation, whenever or wherever it is convenient for the shopper. Location-based shopping offers the expediency of connecting to the Internet wherever for shopping at any place convenient for the shopper.

Retail store restraints of time are also nonexistent with mobile shopping. Most stores are not open 24 hours, seven days a week. Electronic commerce offers this advantage. However, mobile commerce takes round-the-clock shopping to another level. Time is based on convenience of the shopper. No longer is time a shopping constraint. Mobile commerce allows for more time convenience for shopping.

Location. A benefit of mobile commerce is the location of the customer. Everyone is busy—on the go. Shopping on the go refers to immediate purchasing opportunities for consumers so they can make purchasing decisions instantly. Shopping on the go offers retailers the ability to close the sales gap relatively quickly in the consumer decision-making process. When consumers understand their need, search for information, and compare alternatives, a purchase decision is made. Mobile shopping closes the time gap within this process. Immediate purchasing opportunities allow the customer to interact with the retailer without going to an alternate outlet. Immediate purchasing also allows consumers to make a decision without browsing alternative sources. For example, Sarah is shopping for decorative pillows at Local Décor. The Local Décor salesclerk, understanding exactly what Sarah wants, tells her of a shipment coming in a week. The salesclerk shows her pictures of the pillows, allowing Sarah to look at the pictures on her mobile phone, and purchase them from the store, while in the store. By the time the shipment comes to the store, Sarah will have her pillows.

High Level of Ownership. More consumers own mobile phones than any other device. Reaching a target audience is easier and more reliable because most consumers own, have, and are using their mobile devices. Expectations of mobile phone and tablet ownership see continuous rise, however, at a slowing pace.

Individualized Devices. Many consumers either share a desktop computer at home with other family members or use a personal computer at work. In either case, consumers may be reluctant to share information over shared devices. However, mobile phones and most tablets are individually owned and used. Even if a company supplies mobile devices to employees, the devices are not shared. This gives mobile devices personal uniqueness. The consumer, as an individual, is the only user of a mobile device. Messages, communications, and other forms of data can be personalized and exclusive to the individual. For example, Sarah can now receive information from Local Décor, specifically using the colors and items that satisfy Sarah's needs.

Communication between a business and a customer individualized through mobile devices gives each anywhere, anytime convenience. Tablet computers and mobile phone use is frequently specific to one person, even if owned by an employer. Hence, retailers can personalize mobile marketing efforts.

Retailers can reach consumers when convenient for both retailer and for the consumer. When merchandise is first in stock, retailers can reach out to their clientele for quick and easy mobile transactions. In turn, consumers can buy within minutes of a mobile communication from a retailer, whether done while watching television on their tablets, or in another store with their mobile phones.

Profiling customer wants and needs gives retailers the opportunity to sell to whom it makes sense—their target market. Retailers can segment their target to a finite sample and personalize messages, coupons, promotions, and other marketing communications. User-specific information can be gathered allowing for interactivity between the individual and the retailer. Retailers can now focus on distinct customer relationships and offer personal interactions.

Transactions in mobile commerce involve at least one mobile device. For example, a consumer can make a purchase using their tablet computer on an online website. Alternatively, while in a store, a consumer makes a purchase through their mobile phone. This is mobile commerce.

Mobile Devices and Their Roles in Mobile Commerce

A mobile device refers to a handheld device with a computing system that allows for the transfer of voice and/or data transmissions for communication purposes. Wi-Fi, GPS, and Bluetooth allow these devices to connect to the Internet. These devices also run on software called a mobile application, or app. Like software for computers, mobile apps allow users to use their mobile devices as a computer for communication, information, productivity, gaming, and shopping. The two most popular types of mobile devices are mobile (or cell) phones and tablet computers. Mobile consumers use each of these devices. Both mobile phones and tablets run on either an Apple or Android operating system, also referred to as a platform.

Mobile Phones

Although the technology for mobile phones was developed in the early 20th century, the 1973 Motorola portable handset developed by Dr. Martin Cooper was the first commercial cell phone. A large, clunky device, this mobile phone was the first to be used outside of the automobile. It was not until 10 years later that it became commercially produced. In 1992, IBM developed the first smartphone, named Simon, which had not only cell phone capabilities but also a calendar, address book, world clock, calculator, and e-mail capabilities. It was the first cell phone enabled with a touch screen instead of buttons. Several versions of smart phones were developed, including the Windows CE, Palm OS Treo, and Blackberry. Not until the advent of the iPhone in 2007 did consumers began to buy smartphones.

Starting as analog, most mobile phones are now digital, with the advent of wireless networks. There are different types of mobile phones: basic, conventional, and smartphones.

Basic phones allow users to communicate with voice and text. Some offer limited media and the use of keyboards. Prepaid phones and buying minutes prior to use are usually basic. Conventional mobile phones, like basic phones, allow for communication, and also offer Internet access, gaming, and productivity features. However, conventional phones do not allow for the multimedia features of smartphones. Smartphones are to be used as a substitute for a home computer. Smartphones allow users to access the Internet, either through a network or Wi-Fi. The features are advanced with access to a multitude of apps.

Wireless networks allow for computer communications, through radio waves, without a physical connection. Wireless networks now support voice communication, texting, video, and other multimedia at high transmission speeds that rival wired networks.

Mobile Phones and Mobile Commerce. Because of the faster speeds, as well as ubiquitous locations, many consumers prefer to use their mobile phones to desktop computers and laptops for shopping. Mobile phones allow for impulse purchasing as consumers can search pricing while shopping. Mobile phones also give consumers the ability to show others while shopping. For example, when purchasing an expensive item, consumers can send a picture to others for approval before purchase. As a retailer, picture sending is an advantage in being able to close a sale, knowing the consumer sense of the product.

Tablets

Tablet computers are portable devices with touch screen technology. Like mobile phones, tablets allow users portability. Apps are available for productivity, gaming and shopping, as well as multimedia. Unlike mobile phones, tablets are larger and usually take the place of desktop computers and laptops for consumer use. Most have peripherals such as docking stations, keyboards, and a stylus. Tablets offer the best of both desktop computers and mobile phones. Tablets offer larger, touchable screens, and ability to be used anywhere and anytime, and these are personal. Most tablet users spend their evening time shopping online. Tablets make it easier to browse while watching television (Han, Ghose, and Xu 2013).

Tablets and Mobile Commerce. Tablets are most commonly used for shopping by consumers in evenings while watching television. With screen sizes larger than mobile phones, tablets allow consumers the ability to see merchandise as on desktop computers. Many consumers use tablets as substitutes for their desktop computers. Ease of access, convenience, and the ability to browse while lounging gives rise to high levels of shopping on tablet devices. Tablets, like mobile phones, are individual devices, allowing for personalization of products and services by retailers. Consumers are also more likely to spend more when tablet use is coupled with usage of another device (Han, Ghose, and Xu 2013). Tablets are more likely to complement a mobile phone, specifically a smartphone. This is important when retailers develop websites. All sites, regardless of digital device, should be seamless, meaning a unified look and feel, to allow for continuity of service for consumers.

Not only are tablets a channel for consumers, but they are also used by retailers as the point of sale. Tablets are the new cash registers. In order to make the sale anywhere, anytime, retailers are supplying their associates with tablets to ring up sales. Reports state that tablets as payment terminals will increase from 80,000 in 2013 to over two million in 2016 (Evans 2013). Retailers find that using a tablet for sales is less expensive than conventional registers. Sales associates can assist customers with product information, product availability, and check out within minutes. This assistance can reduce checkout line and the possibility of consumer regret before the sale. Smaller retailers have found success with using mobile phones for selling, and now the larger retailers are finding mobile devices can aid in closing sales.

Consumer Considerations for Using Mobile Phones and Tablets

Are desktop computers and laptops going away? Not any time soon. Most consumers will start a shopping task on one device and finish on another. Most will start on a desktop computer or laptop and finishing on a mobile phone or tablet (Han, Ghose, and Xu 2013). Retailers can use this information for a sustainable competitive advantage.

Consumers use technology devices for different tasks. The conundrum of the marketer is understanding these uses and the marketing channels where consumers shop. As shown in Figure 1.1, consumers relate to computer devices in rational and emotional situations. According to Hritzuk and Jones (2014), consumers see the desktop computer as a sage—an intellectual guide for information. Desktop computers are used to make rational shopping decisions. Consumers will look up product information, read reviews, compare prices, and use social media for an understanding before buying. For many consumers, laptops have become substitutes for desktop computers, with portability allowing for ease of

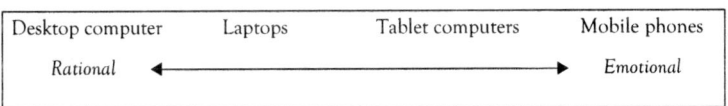

Figure 1.1 Buying decisions based on device

use. However, laptops are generally used in the same manner as desktop computers in information search.

One of the reasons for the increase in mobile shopping is many times consumers use the device at hand when making purchases (Han, Ghose, and Xu 2013). Tablet computers allow consumers to explore on a whim (Hritzuk and Jones 2014). Consumers, while watching television, can buy on impulse, but can also use the tablet to look up product information. For example, a new product commercial may have consumers searching for more information on their tablets, resulting in purchases.

However, when using specifically mobile phones, consumers are more likely to use the device for immediate purchase—a more emotional buy. No product in the store, finding a product that has been researched, using a mobile coupon, or finding a great sale are more emotional buys that are more likely to be done on the mobile phone.

Consumers are more responsive to purchasing when using mobile devices after having researched information online prior to purchase. Mobile devices allow for what seems like impulse purchases, but are actually informed, buy-it-now purchases.

Questions

1. What is digital commerce?
2. What are the benefits of mobile commerce to the consumer, to the retailer?
3. What is the difference between mobile commerce and electronic commerce?
4. What are the three types of mobile phones?
5. Describe the difference between rational and emotional buying.
6. Discuss the implications of using mobile devices for point-of-sale for retailers.

CHAPTER 2

Contrasting E-Commerce and M-Commerce

Why a Digital Commerce Strategy Matters?

Businesses are formed to make money. In order to turn profits, companies develop goals and objectives, and a plan of action to achieve those goals and objectives. Strategy refers to that plan of action a firm conducts in order to define the business and maximize those profits. High-level strategic plans, or business strategies, direct the firm toward meeting organizational goals. Divisional plans within the firm give different levels of the organization that grow the business. However, in order to develop a business strategy, firms must take into account the environments in which to conduct business.

Development of marketing strategies is based on the objectives of the firm, the marketing division, as well as what is happening in the environment. Marketing strategy involves bringing revenues and customers into the firm. Marketing strategy takes into account not only the goals of the organization, but also the business model of the firm, consumer behavior, the marketing mix, competition, and the overall marketplace. One of the aspects that marketing must consider in developing its strategy is digital commerce. Digital commerce initiatives within the firm consist of those strategies that take into account the opportunities and challenges in the marketplace where digital gives the firm a competitive advantage.

In developing a digital commerce strategy, companies consider electronic commerce, mobile commerce, and social commerce. Each, when identified through a SWOT (strengths, weaknesses, opportunities, and threats) analysis, can be found to benefit the strategic goals of the firm. Each plays important but different roles.

- Strengths that the company has in digital commerce
- Weaknesses that the company needs to overcome in digital commerce to stay competitive
- Opportunities that digital commerce affords the company
- Threats from the environment the company must encompass

Many firms bypassed having a mobile commerce strategy for a social commerce. The strengths of the firm were not considered when firms only saw the technological weaknesses. Social commerce is cheaper (in terms of infrastructure). However, when used in conjunction, all of the components of digital commerce can offer gains to both revenue and customers.

Developing a digital commerce strategy means understanding changes in the marketplace and capitalizing on the changes. For example, if the goal of the firm is to increase sales in stores, it makes sense to step back and understand digital shopping behavior. Are your customers using the physical location for purchasing, or is the market moving online? If so, are your customers shopping on the desktop computer, tablet computer, or mobile phone for shopping? Digital commerce strategy aids in generating revenue and developing better relationships with customers in several strategic areas. These areas include

- Brand engagement
- Customer service
- Loyalty programs

Brand Engagement. How engaged is your brand with your audience? Increasing brand awareness and engagement can be accomplished with e-commerce and m-commerce as both allow consumers to engage with brands through more personalized relationships and interactivity. Product reviews dominate brand engagement activities by consumers. Reading product reviews dominates brand-purchasing activities by consumers. E-commerce users are more likely to research the brand, read reviews concerning the brand, and interact with the company through reviews, blogs, forums, e-mail, and website chat sessions. In m-commerce, users are more likely to download apps, or click on mobile websites for product information, immediate purchase, or to locate a specific store featuring a specific brand.

Customer Service. Developing better customer relationships is vital to any firm. Being responsive to customer needs gives firms the opportunity to increase customer support and retention. E-commerce lends itself to customer responsiveness through interactivity such as e-mail support, chat sessions, and detailed product information. M-commerce is vital when customers need quick support, including store location, updated product information, and pricing. In each case, timely responses help build better relationships.

Loyalty Programs. Successful loyalty programs are incorporated into the strategies of many businesses in order to support customers, track program progression, and drive sales—all of which can be done online. Coca-Cola looked to improve its My Coke Rewards program by going mobile. Customers were offered the ability to gain reward points through mobile activities. The program trackers on the mobile website let members know their status and give opportunities to share with other members in the My Coke Rewards community. Although there is no direct mobile purchasing, Coca-Cola used mobile for heightened brand awareness and customer retention.

E-Commerce as a Marketing Strategy

Offering customers the ability to transact business in more than one channel was the purpose of e-commerce, and is now also the purpose of m-commerce. This is not to say that the services offered from each are identical. As there were risks in adopting a multichannel strategy, including cannibalization, technology investment, new alliance associations, new supply chain partners, and the fear that the Internet was just a passing fad (Biyalogorsky and Naik 2003), many of these risks, as well as others are evident in establishing an m-commerce channel.

Although fears of cannibalization were not realized, there is still the perception of the passing fad. Cannibalization refers to lessening of sales in one channel because of the impact of sales in another channel. Some firms felt that too many channels could be harmful, as consumers may not use any channel if there are too many choices. If channel decision becomes another purchase decision, it could turn buyers off.

Established brand name, large customer base, distribution channel, and lower customer acquisition costs gave physical retailers advantages, but these retailers also had large capital investments and limited hours within those physical structures (Enders and Jelassi 2000; White and Daniel 2004). Branding, for example, was the reason for bookstores like Barnes and Noble to establish themselves quickly online. The Internet, on the other hand, has lower entry and establishment costs making it viable as a new marketing channel (Peterson, Balasubramanian, and Bronnenberg 1997) and allowed click only firms, such as Amazon.com, to also start quickly. Many of those first online were more interested in the technology of the Internet, but as online shopping grew, the interest in the Internet as another shopping vehicle abounded.

E-commerce offers retailers opportunities beyond stores. Other products and services such as software, music downloads, insurance, and travel afford the consumer instant gratification. Offering merchandise not found in physical locations, freeing up the costs of inventory, gives consumers a wider variety of products to purchase. Even small town consumers have the ability to purchase merchandise found only in large, metropolitan areas.

E-commerce became popular with retailers once firms realized the Internet's potential as a marketing channel. Implementation of e-commerce increased in competitiveness (Lederer, Mirchandani, and Sims 1997) and found valuable in advancing corporate goals and firm performance. Retailers not only compete with local firms, but global as well. Firms enhance their performance through operational efficiency, automated customer service, greater customer data insight, as well as exchange of information with customers, suppliers, and partners in real-time (Zhuang and Lederer 2006). Exchange of information garners better relationships with stakeholders, strategic alliances as these alliances become market-based assets, tending to be relatively rare and difficult to replicate offline (Srivastava, Fahey, and Christensen 2001). Older, more established retailers developed relationships with newer technology companies, expanding their digital relationships and competitiveness.

Mobile Commerce Strategy and the Marketing Mix

In developing a mobile commerce strategy, consideration of the marketing mix aids in the decision. The marketing mix, or the 4Ps, offers the opportunity to understand the marketplace while bearing in mind the goals and objectives of the firm. What products to sell, how to price products, where to sell products for the target market, and how to promote products are included in the marketing mix. These aspects of marketing can be assessed, not only for marketing as a whole but also in terms of digital commerce. For example, the products sold in the store may be different from those sold online. Alternatively, online promotions may differ from broadcast advertising, which may differ from mobile promotions and advertising. An overall assessment of the goals of the firm should substantiate how the marketing mix is decided and developed. We will give an overview of how mobile fits into this mix.

Product. Product information, or the availability of products, is vital to mobile commerce. Over 28 percent of young adult mobile phone owners use their device to look up reviews while in the store to help their purchase decision (Pew Research Center 2013). Having this information available on a mobile website increases product purchase, not only for young adults, but for executives as well. Seven out of ten executives reported using their mobile device for product information, and many prefer using their tablet for business purchases (Forbes Insights 2013).

Price. Price has more bearing on the effectiveness of mobile commerce than any other portion of the marketing mix. Consumers want the lowest price. Mobile gives them the opportunity to find the lowest price quickly. Best Buy and other retailers were concerned with showrooming, whereby consumers would examine merchandise in the store, check out pricing on their mobile phones, and then purchase elsewhere. However, retailers found that reverse showrooming is more common. Most consumers look for information online, then purchase at the physical location.

Place. Place is anywhere the consumer is located. Place allows the consumer to check product, price, and promotion at any location. Most credit cards are contact based, meaning there has to be physical contact with a machine to read embedded information. With contactless smart cards and smartphones, consumers can tap their phones for payment, coupons, and other in-store offers through a signal that transfers data. Near field communications (NFC), discussed later, makes this type of payment system possible. Credit and debit cards are no longer needed, as information concerning payment is stored in the mobile phone. NFC can be used for product purchases, ticketing, vending machines, restaurants, and other retail establishments. For example, many fast food restaurants allow for mobile ordering whereby consumers preorder, then tap their phones in-store for payment. This procedure allows for quick service for both mobile order and in-line customers.

Promotion. Promoting products and services to individuals is gaining in popularity in m-commerce. Coupons directed toward individuals allows for personalization. Location-based services give retailers the opportunity to offer promotions to those who are nearby.

Firms learned that e-commerce would draw unique customers, and these customers could be attracted to the online channel (Schoenbachler and Gordon 2002). This same understanding is being sought for m-commerce consumers. Benefits of time specificity coupled with geographic distance gives consumers the ability to locate businesses. Understanding mobile consumer behavior allows for better mobile strategy development.

When to purchase, where to purchase, and why purchase have changed with the Internet. Now, mobile commerce has heightened the customer's role in purchase decision-making. With these changes, businesses must also decide how to get their share of revenue in digital commerce.

Business Models

Business models are the ways a firm has for generating revenues. Business models serve as a guide to profit making, based on the firm's goals and objectives. A department store's business model is selling products. A hair salon's business model is selling hair services. A newspaper's business model is based on subscriptions and advertising. The business model can be further refined. Walmart sells products, but at the lowest price possible.

Several different types of business models exist in e-commerce. Some of the more popular business models for E-commerce mimic those models in traditional business environments:

- Bargain discounter
- Brand builders
- Buyer cooperatives
- Dealer support organizations among others.

Sales, advertising, fee assessment, subscriptions, and commissions on sales are basic business models used in e-commerce. Most retailers use a sales business model. Online newspapers, magazines and other content sites rely on subscriptions for revenue. Service transaction firms, such as eBay and investment sites offer their services for a fee.

Many e-commerce business models are unique to the Internet environment. Bundling offers online and offline products in a group to create more value for the users. Cable and telecommunication companies will bundle landline phone, mobile phone, and television services.

Other business models developed because of e-commerce:

- A collaborative consumption business model gives firms the opportunity to use the Internet real-time, or near real-time basis and share profits. Airbnb.com offers worldwide rooming, Uber and Zipcar offer transportation through collaboration with other consumers.
- Offering a basic service and charging for premium services refers to freemium. Sites that offer freemium services include LinkedIn, Dropbox, and Skype.

Based on referring users to a site, affiliate marketing is an add-on business model for many companies online. Using an affiliate model, a retail site will reward other sites when the other sites provide customers to the retail site. For example, a small business owner may have a link to Amazon. When someone on that site clicks on the Amazon link and makes a purchase, the small business owner gets a portion of the proceeds of the sale. This not only brings revenue to the small business owner, but to Amazon as well. Many large corporations offer affiliate marketing for smaller businesses.

Mobile commerce offers firms the opportunity to make a profit, when done effectively. In order to develop a strategy and business model, it is imperative to understand the marketplace. In the early 2000s, the advertising revenue model was popular. Instead of profiting from customers, dotcom companies expected high profits from other companies. However, it was not a stable business model because did not offer a competitive advantage. Now, firms want to enter mobile commerce with a sustainable business model. For now, mobile applications are effective. Many firms are using their e-commerce business models and finding success.

The same e-commerce business models generate revenue on mobile commerce sites. However, the most widely used, and obviously effective business model, has been an elaboration of freemium. The mobile application (or app) is widely used to attract both customers and revenue. The app may be downloaded for free, however, to get the most from the application, or after a period of time, there is a charge for the app. Or, the app is free. However, the user understands that there is a large amount of advertising to endure.

Apps not only allow for revenue building, but data building as well. Data generated through mobile applications allow firms to develop better insight into their customers. In order to download an app, customers must register. Name, address, and other demographic information allows the firm to target advertising, understand the target market, upsell to premium content, and sell products or services. However, free apps come with a lot of churn. Churn refers to subscribers who come and go within a given period. Mobile app users do not feel compelled to continue app usage when investing no money.

Integration of Digital Commerce with Other Business and Marketing Strategies

The integration of digital commerce with other strategies of the firm has not garnered much enthusiasm. Many firms associate digital commerce as its own strategy. In fact, most firms outsource vital Internet functions, as anything digital is considered "too technical" for marketing to handle. However, both e-commerce and m-commerce play vital roles in firms' goals and objectives. Globalization and supply chain are two areas that many companies see as expansion opportunities. Companies looking to expand their customer base globally find starting online can give indications on the possibility with a low financial obligation. Integration of the supply chain allows efficiencies within for all partner companies. Management and coordination of the supply chain through the Internet can make it more productive.

Globalization

E-commerce sales in Asia grew 36 percent in 2014, making this international market twice the size of the U.S. online retail market (Brohan 2015). The European e-commerce grew 15 percent last year. With this growth, many firms are looking to expand their operations globally. Using both e-commerce and m-commerce aid in this expansion as digital commerce is an effective and efficient means of globalization.

The reach of the Internet allowed retailers to expand globally, overcoming obstacles of time and communication. Several advantages afforded those retailers that decided on a global e-commerce strategy. Hamill (1997) suggested that the future of international Internet commerce should lead to international price standardization, reduction of intermediaries, and an effective medium for worldwide market research Further, the Internet has significant potential in satisfying customer demand on a global level (Jones, Clarke-Hill, and Hillier 2002).

In looking at the globalization of e-commerce through internationalization theory, Kim, Suh, and Hwang (2003) posited that gradual internationalization was better for sociocultural distance than just cultural distance, even though the process was rapid with the Internet. As firms gradually move globally, their perceived risk diminishes (Kim, Suh, and Hwang 2003). With websites available 24 hours a day and translated into other languages with translation software, retailers were able to reach out to new international markets (Erdem and Utecht 2002), including small and medium-sized enterprises (Haas 2002). The main reason firms engaged in online international retailing were relationship facilitation, information, as well as transactions in international markets (Arnott and Bridgewater 2002).

Retailers who integrated global activities with their overall marketing and corporate strategies gained more effectiveness of e-commerce than those who did not extend globally (Doherty, Ellis-Chadwick, and Hart

2003). There are now several barriers to the globalization of m-commerce; specifically, the nature of the telecommunications industry worldwide.

The diffusion of mobile devices began more extensively in Europe and Asia than in the United States. In a contrast between American buyers (an individualistic culture) and South Koreans (a collective culture), Park and Jun (2003) found no significant differences in Internet shopping experience, though the perceived risks were higher in Korea (Park and Jun 2003). This difference afforded firms the desire to go global in terms of customers. More than 13 percent of global consumers use mobile devices for online shopping, with smartphones preferred over tablets (Callard 2014). In both Japan and South Korea, m-commerce accounts for more than 45 percent of retail transactions (Criteo 2014).

In several studies discussing consumer behavior Phau and Poon (2000) compared potential Internet buyers and nonbuyers in Singapore finding, as in the United States, that expensive goods like cars were not ready for online sales because of the monetary risks involved. Most of the purchasing done for products frequently purchased had a low outlay. Globalization in m-commerce may mean going country-by-country, as was done in traditional retailing, until there is cohesion in global technology. Future research can determine, and assess the diffusion of m-commerce. Until there is a diffusion of mobile capabilities globally, the advantages of worldwide mobile commerce will not be met. All the players within the supply chain will only satisfy customer demand on a global level after the technology is not only in place, but also in use.

Supply Chain Integration

Business-to-business revenues are twice those of business-to-consumer revenues (Hoar 2012), making B2B a viable channel for both e-commerce and m-commerce. Electronic commerce has enabled supply chain partners to reduce costs, allowing the savings passed to consumers. Internet, as well as an extranet, provide ease in transactions, quick and updated information, reduced costs, and closer buyer/seller relationships.

During the 2013 holiday season, many deliveries were delayed. Many Christmas gifts were late and people were upset. Although bad weather was blamed by UPS, FEDEX, and the U.S. Postal Service, consumers faulted the delivery companies for the late deliveries. A breakdown in the supply chain was the culprit.

Resources that firms have developed through electronic commerce include technological applications and relationships, both business and consumer. Capabilities include the knowledge gained through these technologies and relationships. Technology is not only changing how we live, but these same technologies are changing how firms conduct business. How these technologies incorporate themselves into corporate strategies and provide revenues are questions to be answered by the firms.

Other companies are taking advantage of m-commerce abilities in order to develop new technologies. In order to make web surfing easier on mobile phones, the .mobi domain name for wireless web pages has been made available for companies to design pages specifically for wireless devices (Yuan 2006).

The ability to update pricing and product information online gives suppliers and buyers easy access to data in order to make quicker, more informed decisions. Companies no longer send salespersons to clients as often, lessening travel costs, as online meetings can be just as productive. The relationships between clients and salespersons can still be purposeful, as well as efficient, as online communications saves time.

Rim In Motion was one of the first companies to understand the value of mobile in supply chain communications. Marketing to a B2B audience, Blackberry was introduced to companies to communicate with other companies. Outfitting firms with their Blackberry mobile devices, many companies that were just beginning to understand e-commerce within the supply chain were now about to realize how mobile could integrate partners. Going beyond pages, supply chain partners could now exchange e-mails anywhere, anytime. Salespersons and other business people could stay connected on the road. It was once said that if Blackberry went out of business, so does the U.S. government, as it became the communication device of choice.

Now, with smartphones and tablets, supply chain operations can be used to optimize routing, assess inventory quickly, transmit orders, verify orders, scan code information, and communicate with anyone in the chain.

Through mobile communications, routes can be changed depending upon traffic, weather conditions, and other obstacles. Responsive logistics refers to the ability to be flexible and adjust the supply chain through hurdles while still delivering as close to on time as possible. Mobile allows responsive capability. Customer demand, damaged products, and other problems can impede inventory controls. Mobile communication allows for quick response to inventory management challenges for rapid replenishment.

Tablets have replaced not only desktop computers, but clipboards as well. Tablets allow supply chain personnel, especially those within warehouse operations, to retrieve information, read purchase orders, check inventories, develop invoices, print shipping labels, and track order processing.

Three types of systems are used in transmitting large data in a small format:

- Barcodes
- Quick response codes (QR)
- Radio frequency ID tags (RFID)

Once scanned, barcodes allow for speedy access to product and other information. As QR codes are specific to mobile devices, all are useful in mobile commerce. RFID tags are beneficial in tracking large quantities of goods as the tags can be placed on large boxes and palettes. Bar code technology is allowing cell phone users to download information for items while shopping. Barcodes aid in managing inventory to know what is available, improve efficiency by reducing data entry errors, and improve transaction accuracy. Mobile devices all along the supply chain can scan each so that anyone can gain the information needed in real time. All of these activities impact the consumer as a robust supply chain maximizes efficiency and passing costs along to the end customer.

Questions

1. What should marketing departments take into account when developing strategy?
2. What can digital strategy accomplish for the firm?
3. Explain how to incorporate mobile commerce within the marketing mix.
4. Name three types of e-commerce business models.
5. Why is digital commerce important to the firm's strategy to grow globally?
6. How does mobile commerce impact supply chain integration?

CHAPTER 3

What Connects the Target?

In the beginning of electronic commerce, competition came from both click-only companies, as well as other brick-and-mortar companies, so firms found it necessary to develop an online presence. The first retailers online who did venture forth found the Internet had given them a competitive advantage over those that remained entirely brick-and-mortar. Click-and-mortar companies found a new consumer market, those who were unable to be brick-and-mortar customers because of time or space, or those who liked the opportunity to shop online.

Many large retailers were reluctant to develop an online presence because of the fear of cannibalization. In essence, their customers would stop going to the stores and only shop online, leaving retailers with expensive real estate and no profits. What these retailers failed to understand was their target market. Those who would shop in the stores continued. These customers also began to shop online, and now on mobile devices. However, online, and now mobile, has spawned segments of shoppers that stores fail to attract.

In determining the segment, retail establishments study those who would frequent within a market area. For example, if higher income families heavily populate a location, more likely stores and restaurants that cater to upscale consumers will develop in the area. Location in e-commerce, though, is different. Upscale consumers can still be the target, yet their location is different. Many marketers have recently found their upscale market online in China. Same segment, different location. However, the target market is different.

Defining a target market may seem easy, but targeting the right market can take time. College students are NOT a target market. Homemakers are NOT a target market. College students and homemakers are segments of the population. Capturing the essence of college students or homemakers can lead to the development of a target market. Are the college students attending a university or community college? Are they living in a dorm or commuting? Are the homemakers young mothers or empty nesters? Do they have young children or taking care of aging parents? Each has different buying needs and wants. Each is different in where and how they buy.

M-commerce takes targeting to another level. Targeting becomes granular. It is not just about the location where the target lives, but the target in and around the purchasing location.

Consumers are motivated to shop online because it is convenient, it is different, and increases the variety of products available. Depending upon the person or situation, motivations to shop online motivations can be utilitarian (need), or hedonic reasons (fun). Lowest price for a product is important, but many online shoppers just prefer surfing. For those who shop online, they are usually shopping lovers, tech lovers, or just browse for the adventure (Brengman et al. 2005).

Money and time drive convenience for consumers. Finding the lowest price takes time, but offers the convenience of saving money. Money-conscious shoppers like e-commerce. These consumers spend time online researching for the lowest price, whether it is the product price, shipping cost, or other monetary choices. e-Marketer (2015) finds that travel research and booking is still primarily on desktops (52 percent).

Time-conscious shoppers are more likely going to use m-commerce. Price is an essential component to their shopping experience; however, these consumers want to make a quick purchasing decision. Mobile coupons and online price comparisons aid consumers who want both types of convenience when shopping on their mobile devices. However, ultimately consumers want a website, no matter what the device, which is convenient to navigate quickly, containing the information (or content) that makes their search expedient.

Digital Content

Content is king—the new mantra of marketing departments has implications beyond royalty. Content is information. Customers, to make better purchasing decisions, use information. The Internet has enabled

Table 3.1 E-commerce and M-commerce content types

Types of content		
Website articles	Mobile site	Image captions
Videos	Infographics	Mobile apps
Blog posts	Tweets	Facebook posts
Instagram captions	Advertising	Promotional materials
White papers	Research reports	Media mentions
Press releases	Podcasts	Product information
Newsletters	e-mail	Slide presentations

consumers to find information when needed. No longer do buyers have to wait until a trip to the auto dealer to learn about cars. Consumers can look up competitive pricing information while in-store. Information, or content, is now readily available and is now convenient. However, the lack of relevant content, inconsistency between online and mobile site content, and content that is not optimized for quick searches are making consumers unhappy with most websites. Table 3.1 highlights some of the content found on e-commerce and m-commerce sites.

Content allows marketers to relate with customers in various ways. Content allows engagement, interaction, information, and a defined call to action.

In developing content, an understanding of the user is pertinent as well as reasons for content. In short, content

- solves a problem—understand why the user needs the information
- is effective—content should move the consumer along the path to purchase
- is concise—deliver content quickly and efficiently
- targets the user—focus content on your market and their needs
- fits the channel—content should be appropriate to the website, social site, or mobile application
- is consistent—content should have the same message throughout each marketing channel

Websites: The Key to the Consumer

Of all visits to websites, 53 percent were from mobile devices (Branding Brand Mobile Commerce 2015). In 2014, the share of visits from desktops and laptops dropped from 18 to 15 percent. Interestingly, the share of visits from tablets dropped as well (17 percent), while the share for smartphones increased 41 percent.

Forbes Insights (2013) found that while mobile is useful for their positions, most executives do not use mobile devices for purchasing because of difficulty in navigating through mobile websites and apps. Most preferred using tablets for searching for product information; using their mobile device for purchasing would be the natural next step. In fact, executives would prefer purchasing on mobile devices, both tablets and smartphones, if it were easier to do so.

Consumers like a virtual environment that is similar to a retailer's physical structure for a reference point (Wikström, Carlell, and Frostling-Henningsson 2002). The look and feel of a website should emulate that of the store. Incompatibility keeps many shoppers from shopping on websites because of confusion on the part of consumers. If a website does not complement the look and feel of what the shopper expects, the attitude toward that website may be negative. For example, an upscale department store should have an upscale website presence. Consumers do not expect to view savings information on an upscale website. Designer products and fashion updates should be present on the website, as in the store. Now, consumers expect this same compatibility for mobile websites and applications.

Usability and interactivity attract consumers to websites (Constantinides 2004); content keeps them interested and purchasing. Usability refers to the ease of using a website, including easy navigation, updated links, and quick loading. Interactivity is responsiveness through human-to-human or human-to-computer interactions. Consumers will spend more time on sites, that are usable and interactive. Hence, the longer time someone is online, the more likely they are to shop online (Lohse, Bellman, and Johnson 2000).

Browsers perceived considerably more financial, time, and psychological risks on e-commerce websites than heavy or moderate shoppers, whereas moderate shoppers mere more likely to perceive product performance risk, and heavy shoppers perceived less overall risk (Forsythe and Shi 2003). However, sites that attracted bargain seekers do not have high repeat purchasers (Reibstein 2002). Sites that take advantage of low prices may only attract the most price-sensitive customers, those that lack loyalty, or bargain seekers (Reibstein 2002). Chandon, Morwitz, and Reinartz (2004) studied repeat purchasing behavior in terms of intentions, finding that the likelihood of repeat purchasing declined over time after the first purchase.

Marketers who use mobile devices for marketing purposes are finding difficulty in transferring e-commerce website design. In fact, there are many inherent problems with mobile devices, keeping mobile from the explosive new technology that everyone was hoping mobile marketing would become.

Small screens, tiny keypads, and limited battery life are some of the inadequacies that consumers find when using mobile phones, and other mobile devices. Moreover, though it sounds strange, the big finger syndrome is responsible for wrong key strokes in transactions and typing. The small size of the mobile device screen, though it is getting larger, is still too small for some graphics and images for websites. Lastly, the attention span of those on a mobile device is shorter than those using a desktop computer. Understanding this restraint, website design, navigation, and the buying process must be taken into account.

Most consumers find that mobile websites do not give enough content. Even if the mobile website is easy to navigate, the lack of content makes the sites inadequate (SalesForce 2014).

Google research (2012) found that most consumers (74 percent) would return to a site that is mobile-friendly, and more likely to buy (67 percent) from that site. On the other hand, 61 percent would go to another site if they could not find what they were looking for right away. In addition, 96 percent found that most of the mobile websites they encountered were not designed for mobile devices. Many felt frustrated and annoyed (48 percent) and felt they wasted their time (36 percent) and less likely to engage with the company (52 percent).

The impact of these challenges has led marketers to find the ideal atmosphere in which to conduct business in the mobile market. Because mobile marketing encompasses advertising, commerce, as well as promotion, the ideal servicescape, or physical environment, must be able to overcome the challenges mentioned previously for all mobile marketing purposes.

Atmospherics, how the site looks and feels, are as important to virtual commerce as store layout is to traditional retailers, if not more so. Atmospherics refers to the designing of space to create a positive purchase environment that may enhance the likelihood of purchase (Kotler 1973–1974). The characteristics of a website, like a retail establishment, influence consumers' shopping behavior (Menon and Kahn 2002). This includes the environment of an online retail establishment, which has been found to affect consumers' desire to purchase, though conventional retail store layout did not apply to a virtual retail layout (Vrechopoulos et al. 2004).

Atmospherics are as important to virtual commerce as store layout is to traditional retailers, if not more so. The relationship between the retailer and the consumer is an important element that cannot be offered in other channels (Kolesar and Galbraith 2000) and must be satisfied by the online retailer through the capacity for direct personal interaction. As the traditional retail outlet has changed over time, the online shopping experience has moved toward atmospheres that have their own cues for customer satisfaction. Some of these have come from the traditional store whereas others have come from the online experience itself. These are likely be the way in which mobile commerce atmospherics will manifest itself in the time to come.

Customers tend to judge a website in terms of quality and satisfaction in terms of its design, reliability in fulfillment, privacy and security concern, and customer service (Wolfinbarger and Gilly 2003). Novak, Hoffman, and Yung (2000) suggested that the activities involved in product search do not yet offer levels of challenge and arousal for a compelling online customer experience. Although touch and feel are important to the experience for consumers when purchasing products (Li, Daugherty, and Biocca 2001), an online experience can still be positive with the interactivity that the Internet offers.

Mobile Applications

In connecting to the Internet, consumers spend 12 percent of their time browsing and 88 percent of their time with mobile apps (IAB 2014).

Mobile applications, or apps, have become increasingly important in mobile commerce for both businesses and consumers. Developed for both Apple and Android platforms, apps are software downloads for mobile devices. That is the good news. The bad—every company has an app. The iPhone App Store launched in July 2008 with 800 apps, and by September 2014, there were over 1.3 million apps available. Apps have become the principal method for information dissemination in mobile. Specific to smartphones and tablets, apps are downloadable software, usually bearing the logo, or other brand identification.

Mobile apps have a high level of user engagement, which can translate into a more positive attitude and personal connection toward a brand (Bellman et al. 2011). Companies are enthusiastic about developing apps in order to maximize the impact of brand awareness. Hence, the excessive number of apps on the market—both free and priced. Not only is the number of apps growing, but also the time spent with apps is increasing.

Starbucks, which has been the mobile marketer for several years, integrates mobile commerce within their app for 13 million users for over 6 million mobile apps weekly. Mobile transactions represent over 16 percent of the company's total transactions. Starbucks customers can order, track their loyalty program, and pay through their Starbucks app. Customers have shorter wait times and a better in-store experience when using the app. Starbucks is using the app to introduce express locations to streamline the purchase even more.

Some of the preferences for using apps over the mobile web (IAB 2014) include

- More convenient
- Easy to use
- Ability to use when the mobile device is not connected to the Internet

Those who prefer the web did not want to spend money to purchase apps, were disappointed in the apps downloaded, and found the web browser easier to use. Others found apps took up too much space on their devices and too much time to download.

Other problems with mobile apps include lack of retention and abandonment. Downloading does not equate to usage. According to

Localytics, in 2014 20 percent of apps were used only once, while usage of apps over 10 times climbed to 39 percent, indicating app retention is increasing. Retaining the app is more likely for those who purchase an app. However, abandoning an app, or app churn, is higher when users do not return to the app within seven days of downloading. In fact, 60 percent of users never returned if the app was not used within seven days of downloading. Keeping this in mind, firms should market their apps in order to increase usage to those downloading within the first seven days. Yet, if the app does not contain content, design, and usability, no marketing efforts will be sufficient.

There are many uses for apps for mobile commerce. Facilitating better customer engagement, apps can address needs and wants in terms of shopping. Apps are your business. Apps tell customers who you are and how you are going to assist them. Apps should not create problems, but offer solutions to problems and challenges. Apps should answer the question *How do I?* Apps should offer value to both the customer and the business, as shown in Table 3.2.

Table 3.2 Value of mobile apps

What customers need	What you gain
Advertising	Sales
Promotions	Loyal customers
Customer service	Engaged customers
Product/service information	Leads
Pricing information	Relationships
Loyalty programs	Immediacy
Payments	New customers
Pre-ordering/ordering	Customer data
Couponing and discounts	Brand awareness
Make reservations	Competitive advantage
Location-based services	Targeted customers
Shopping lists	
Personalization	
Time savings	
Purchasing flexibility	
Comparison shopping	

Responsive Design

Consumers react positively to websites and applications with informational content, hassle-free navigation, and appealing design. Users will immediately abandon a site if it causes them to react negatively to site usage. Responsive design refers to optimizing sites and apps taking into account movement through the space, layout, coloring, fonts, and usability. Coalescence of all that the site offers should invite users to respond to offers, read content, make purchases, chat with staff, and recommend the site to others. Users want sites and apps that respond to their needs and behaviors.

Responsive design takes into account the environment of the site. Putting a catalog online as an e-commerce website does not work. Taking the e-commerce site and shrinking it for m-commerce does not work. Taking a mobile phone app and calling it a tablet website does not work. Nuances of different devices call for distinctions in their development.

Originally fashioned for information technology developers, responsive design took into account the architecture of websites and applications. However, responsive design is pertinent to marketers as well.

E-commerce websites should be designed to take advantage of the space available. Monitors range in size, with some using two monitors at one time. Large images, several frames, bold colors, lots of text can be used to fill space. M-commerce websites and applications do not have the advantage of space. In fact, because of the shortage of space, designing for mobile, various screen sizes must be taken into account.

Use of keyboards, phone pads, and touchscreens affects design. Cursor-based devices have different structures. Touchscreens do not support hovering, changing from a pointer to a hand when hovering over a link before clicking. Spacing links so that fingers do not touch the wrong link is imperative. Tap targets must be placed in what is known as thumbzones—where the thumb rests on the mobile device. Screen orientation should be taken into account. Can the mobile site rotate depending on the orientation of the screen? A fluid layout should have the ability to switch from portrait to landscape mode. Load times need to be shorter to take into account battery life of the device and Wi-Fi connections. Color support varies by device, meaning sharpness and brightness of images will differ. In addition, for all sites, content should be optimized for search engines. Ensure your content is properly displayed, succinct yet to the point, and stresses location, as most mobile searches are local.

Lastly, design sites for cohesiveness. Online websites, smartphone websites, tablet websites, and mobile applications should have the same look, feel, design that attracts customers to your business. Colors, fonts, images, and other design features should combine so that customers know they are doing business with you no matter the device. Develop a theme that is consistent throughout all development and marketing efforts. Cohesiveness not only aids in search engine optimization, but also allows customers to move fluidly throughout your digital spaces.

Questions

1. Explain the difference between a segment and a target.
2. Describe the target for the following sites: clubpenguin.com, thirdage.com, disneyparks.com
3. Explain the difference between money-conscious and time-conscious consumers.
4. Find a mobile application that is free, but also offers a freemium. What are the differences?
5. Why is content "king"?
6. Find an e-commerce website and a mobile website for a company. Compare and contrast the sites. Explain in terms of responsive design.

CHAPTER 4

Touchpoints

Where Is the Elusive Digital Consumer?

There are many digital touchpoints and the numbers are on the rise. Touchpoints refers to any connection point a company has with a customer. Touchpoints can be face-to-face, when a customer enters a store, or during a personal selling encounter. Content touchpoints include a catalog, mailer, flyer, or advertisement. Websites, online videos, and mobile apps are just a few digital touchpoints.

Human interaction, physical interaction, digital interaction, self-service technology interactions—all are touchpoints. All are areas of interaction in which a company can make a connection with a customer. All are areas in which customers decide whether to continue along their path to purchase in a shopping experience. Any connection with a customer is a touchpoint. Touchpoints, as you can see, are extremely important points of contact, and are to be considered as such in developing any connection made with a customer or potential customer. Consumers become less accepting of poor service when moving through touchpoints. Long lines, intolerant employees, slow navigation, stockouts, and poor ambience through channels will chase customers away (Rigby 2011).

Listed in Table 4.1 are several digital customer touchpoints. This list is not exhaustive. There are many ways to connect with customers, and potential customers, in both e-commerce and m-commerce. Many of these areas can be broken down even further. For example, a website includes the home page, landing page, product information pages, shopping cart, and so on. Some areas overlap, and others are distinct. However, all are valuable in linking with buyers.

Table 4.1 Digital touchpoints

E-commerce touchpoints	M-commerce touchpoints
B2C website	Mobile website
B2B website	Tablet website
Software	Mobile application
Live chat	Tablet application
E-mail	Voice communication
Video conferencing	Text messaging
Affiliates	Social media
Advertising	Affiliate applications
Social media	E-mail
Company blogs	Live chat
Third party blogs	Advertising
News	QR codes
Webinars	Search results
Loyalty programs	Loyalty programs
Search results	Customer service
Customer service	Third-party retail (i.e., Amazon)
Third-party retail (i.e., Amazon)	Product reviews
Product reviews	Delivery
Delivery	Mobile promotions
Online promotions	Games
Games	Landing pages
Landing pages	Shopping carts
Shopping carts	

Each touchpoint has its own impact on the path to purchase. All have impact, all are important, all add value to the consumer, and all should be considered in cooperation and not in isolation. There are points in which the company can control. Websites, applications, promotions, advertising, and other areas the company develops are controllable. Other touchpoints such as product reviews, third-party blogs, and news articles are still significant along the consumer's path to purchase, even if the firm is unable to deliver the content.

In looking at specific touchpoints, both online and mobile, you can get a sense of what attracts customers to that touchpoint, and how to develop that point of contact for maximum effectiveness.

Website

Customers come to your website because they *want* to. Unlike a television commercial, where someone watches because it is there, contact with an e-commerce website is for a specific purpose. The previous chapter explains how to achieve a successful website—overall. However, specific portions of the website may go unnoticed by a marketer, yet are important to the customer. These touchpoints are valuable and should be treated as such. Map your customer's journey through your site. Navigate your website as a customer and answer the following questions.

- What is missing?
  - o What are customers looking for that is not meeting their needs?
- What is not working?
  - o Are all page links working properly and navigating to the right pages?
- What is out of date?
  - o Is all of your information correct and timely?

Now, develop your site, content, and links to the ultimate experience for your customers. Here are a few pointers for specific digital touchpoints.

E-mail

E-mail is a vital way to stay in contact with a customer. It is a two-way communication. E-mail garners interaction that supersedes the transaction process. This touchpoint is very special because approval has already been granted before you can send an e-mail to a customer. Either by opting in or opting out, e-mail is consent-based, giving you permission to use e-mail as a touchpoint. If a customer has opted to receive e-mails from your company, then your customer wants to hear from you.

Keep this relationship positive by using these reminders:

1. Send e-mails that provide important information such as specific product pricing.
2. Let customers feel special by providing deals for select customers.
3. As in any relationship, do not overuse your access.
4. Stay top of mind, but do not flood inboxes. You will find yourself in the spam folder.

Marketing Automation

Presetting your marketing efforts allows you to send e-mails at specific times, to specific audiences using software technology that systematizes the e-mail process. Marketing automation allows for more effective and efficient mailings at defined times. Using customer relationship management systems, marketers can sell, upsell, and deliver content to those quantified in the company data systems. Large companies combine IT and marketing departments to develop an automated system. Smaller companies can use software or e-mail marketing companies for this process.

E-mail customers expect special treatment. Automated marketing systems generates e-mails to allow for distinctive treatment, sending them to landing pages, instead of the homepage, that make their journey through either your website or mobile site a delight. A landing page is a page that has a link from our e-mail to a specific product or information. Give them content on the landing page that makes them feel like no one else is receiving this special information. Invite them to specials, webinars, in-store activities, and online events. Use e-mail to develop and maintain relationships with those who want a connection with you.

Blog

A blog should not be another e-commerce page. Customers do not want to be sold in a blog. Customers expect interaction, information, and a sense of community. A blog is a cross between a relaxed corporate site and a social site. It should be information, informal, and fun. Though a blog can be an online site, it should also be developed as a tablet or smartphone site as well. Availability at all times is key for all sites. Blogs are friendly. A blog is a touchpoint that allows for a friendship between a company and its public. Use it as in informal setting for a conversation. A blog is transparent. Let customers post their comments. Always respond to their comments. No one wants to be ignored. A customer who is snubbed on a blog feels the company is distant and not really wanting to get to know their customers on a personal level. Use a blog as an entry point to social networking.

Loyalty Programs

Encouraging customers to purchase on a regular basis is the objective of most loyalty programs. Frequent shopping behaviors tallied with points allows for discounts, freebies, and other rewards through the use of loyalty cards and other systems. Online advantages include the ability to track points for both the marketer and the customer. Loyalty cards and keytags can be used for offline purchases. However, wisdom suggests giving customers the ability to earn points for online purchases by giving them the ability to add either a card number or a telephone number. When given ability to use a loyalty program when purchasing online, customers are more likely to purchase knowing they are making advances toward discounts or free merchandise.

Loyalty programs can also be partnered with nonprofit organizations. When a customer purchases from a retailer, proceeds can be donated to the customer's choice of nonprofit organization. A loyalty program not only enhances purchasing, but also boosts commitment to both the retailer and the nonprofit by the customer.

Shopping Carts

Shopping carts are a very vital touchpoint. Shopping carts gene making the sale quick rate revenue. Conversion of browsers to buyers is the goal of shopping carts. Customers decide either to buy or to abandon at the shopping cart, and many factors aid in their decision. Some of these influences include:

- Shipping costs—many will abandon the cart if the total exceeds what they were planning to spend.
- Payment options—lack of a specific type of credit or debit card, or not wanting to use an electronic payment service.
- Price—possible coupons, discounts, or understanding of competitive pricing.
- Credibility of the website—any problems in trying to check out may preclude a customer from continuing a sale.

Many of these are also factors when shopping in an offline store. However, customers online may abandon a cart for a myriad of other reasons—distractions, shopping while working, or disruption in Internet service.

To alleviate as many disruptions to the continuance of the purchasing decision, offer customers information prior to the sale. Transparency in pricing gives customers better alternatives in shopping. Many retailers now offer the opportunity to see the shipping costs prior to the purchase. This gives the customer alternatives with a variety of cost options.

Allow customers to use coupons and gift cards throughout the purchasing process. For example, once an item is placed in the cart, an option for a discount, coupon or other offer can be used. Therefore, the discounted price is seen, giving the customer a better sense of what will be the actual price.

Mobile shopping carts can pose unique challenges to customers. Simplicity is key, as the purchase decision has been made. Less content, and more responsiveness to the checkout process is key. Use those fields that are vital to the checkout process, making the sale quick, focused, and streamlined.

Text Messages

Text messaging can be a wonderful way to interact with customers. Text messaging is personal, it is immediate, it is on target with the message, and it is short. It is also cheap. When using text messaging first make sure you have permission. Text messaging allows you to privately converse with your customers.

Customers like to use text messaging for customer support. Text messaging is also a great resource for sending reminders, confirmations, and alerts. However, text messages are bothersome when the message comes unexpectedly and too frequently. Time your text messaging as not to annoy. Show value in any text message you send to a customer.

How ISPs Affect E-Commerce Touchpoints

Consumers are not fond of their Internet service providers (ISPs). Customer satisfaction reports usually place ISPs near the bottom. Disruption of service, rate hikes, and poor customer service are just some of the problems consumers report. How does this affect your website?

If a customer is involved in a purchase, a disruption of service may impede online transactions. The customer may abandon the sale depending on the timing and length of the disruption.

Rate hikes may cause customer churn not only for the ISP but also for online businesses. When a customer terminates an ISP, their e-mail address is also discontinued. These changes in e-mail addresses may interrupt your contact with a particular customer. Customers may or may not update their information, and may become to you a lost customer.

Also, make sure that your website is compatible with major browsers as well. Nothing is more disappointing than to read, "This website is not compatible with your particular browser." If most of your customers use either Firefox or Google Chrome, make sure your website is well suited for these particular browsers. Long wait times, or worse, not working with these browsers at all will keep customers from your site. Test your website in all major browsers to make sure the site works properly in terms of loading and navigation.

How Mobile Suppliers Affect M-Commerce Touchpoints

Just as an ISP delivers a website, the mobile supplier also affects mobile Internet. The type of smartphone, the delivery of the Internet service, as well as the mobile application touch the consumer.

Smartphones are structured for maximum communications usability—both voice and data. Users should be able to talk, type, use apps, use the Internet, text message, take pictures, calculate, navigate, and e-mail in one handheld device. However, in order to operate a smartphone, customers must be connected to a network provided by a wireless provider, usually a telecommunications company.

In terms of coverage, any type of computer network that uses wireless data connections can provide wireless coverage. Wi-Fi coverage can be found in homes, citywide, campus-wide, airports, hotels, restaurants, just about anywhere. Within the past few years, Wi-Fi coverage has become free for consumer use and provides Internet access within the range of the wireless network. Wireless coverage is usually rather stable. However, dropping coverage between nodes can cause disruptions.

Social Touchpoints: E-Commerce and M-Commerce Opportunities

Consumers are likely to use social media both electronically and on mobile devices. Social media gives marketers several touchpoints that connect with their customers. As consumers have become more comfortable interacting with businesses on social media, these touchpoints can become opportunities for sales, service, loyalty programs, and new customers.

Facebook

Consumers connect with Facebook on almost every device. Marketers that tried to use Facebook as a sales tool were met with objections. However, this social site gives the opportunity to interact with influencers, announce new opportunities, and understand marketplace buzz. Facebook gives businesses the opportunity to relax, unwind, and converse with their customers. As a touchpoint, consumers can interact with a business at any time. Photos and videos on Facebook can show interactions with products, whereby consumers can see the products in action.

Twitter

A tweet is an outlet for businesses to post information that can be spread immediately. Want to get customers to your commerce sites quickly? Add interest by tweeting information. Like Facebook, consumers use Twitter on most electronic and mobile devices. A tweet sends the message that the information is fresh. Use the opportunity to connect with customers and potential customers to boost sales. Make sure to direct them to the correct landing page with a shortened URL to get the maximum out of a small number of characters.

LinkedIn

Many marketers forget LinkedIn as a customer touchpoint. LinkedIn provides the opportunity for customers to know your company at a higher level. For customers looking for a company that sells business-to-business, or even more expensive business-to-consumer products, LinkedIn is a viable alternative to the proverbial "About Us" webpage. LinkedIn allows for a connection, an interaction, and a way for introductions.

As with other social media, LinkedIn connections occur through both electronic and mobile devices. Maximize this social outlet by keeping the status of your company and connections updated.

Video: Traversing All That Is Digital

Marketing through video is becoming a viable, as well as vital, touch point to customers. Videos give customers a view of your company, products, and brand conveniently, which can be short and fun. Videos can be posted on most social sites, allowing customers to interact from other touchpoints.

The types of videos can range from short 10-second commercials to longer webinars and tutorials. Video can drive customers to your retail outlet or commerce site because of its engagement. Video marketing allows for show and tell. Videos give the opportunity to promote a new product, remind customers of a product, or educate consumers on the use of a product.

As YouTube can be a viable platform for a video, also remember that consumers view videos on most social media as well as web and mobile sites. Videos can also go viral, giving the opportunity to spread throughout the marketplace. Most consumers like videos and are more likely to become engaged than with text because video is easy to watch. Video gets attention quickly. Video is memorable. Video also gives the opportunity for storytelling.

Storytelling in a video involves consumers through vignettes. Videos with stories can be used to promote, engage, educate, or just entertain. Storytelling engages the listener by making a point that is valued in an easy to understand format (Lundqvist et al. 2013). A story can create positive associations with a company, brand, or product, which can increase a consumer's willingness to buy (Lundqvist et al. 2013).

Search Engine Optimization (SEO): Making Sure There Is a Touchpoint

Consumers most likely reach online and mobile websites either by typing in the URL or through a search engine. Compatibility of the URL with the name of the company, brand, and product is important in finding a site and going through a search engine. A search engine result is a touchpoint. You want to assure that your website and mobile rank high on all of the major search engines: Google, Bing, Yahoo, and Ask as well as AOL, WebCrawler, and DuckDuckGo.

When developing a search engine marketing plan, remember customers will be coming to both your website and mobile site. Optimize and advertise for both sites.

Make sure that keywords associated with your sites are used frequently and not overused. Most websites contain the necessary keywords and phrases. However, in order to keep sites small, many mobile sites lack the necessary words and phrases needed to be effective in a search.

Questions

1. Name five e-commerce touchpoints.
2. Name five m-commerce touchpoints.
3. Discuss the value of touchpoints to customer interaction.
4. How does telling a story in a video affect customer touchpoints?
5. Explain how SEO affects digital touchpoints.

CHAPTER 5

Challenges to Digital Commerce

Improving the Digital Shopping Experience

Consumers have different shopping needs. Consumers also have different shopping options. Shopping with others or alone. Online searching, talking with employees, reading reviews. Large assortment of products, niche products, customized products. Digital, in store, catalog, mail order, television. To accommodate shopping needs, business offers consumers varying ways of shopping. However, retailers and consumers look at these channels differently. Retailers have a multichannel view, whereas consumers have an omnichannel view of the shopping experience.

Multichannel Marketing

The capability of offering the purchasing of products from more than one channel refers to multichannel marketing. Multichannel marketing allows for the enhancement of service for consumers to enrich their satisfaction (Wallace, Giese, and Johnson 2004), as well as value in offering them the ability to use different channels (Noble, Griffith, and Weinberger 2005). Brick and mortar allows for a social shopping experience, as well as tactility in purchasing. Catalogs and televisions afford the comfort of shopping at home. E-commerce has the benefits of shopping at home, as well as an interactive experience. M-commerce gives consumers the benefits of all channels, including anywhere, anytime shopping. Although the main purpose of both retailing online and offline is consumer purchasing, each has its own advantages and disadvantages. According to Christensen and Tedlow (2000), "the essential mission of retailing has always had four elements: getting the right product in the right place at the right price at the right time." Established brand name, large customer base, distribution channel, and lower customer acquisition costs give physical retailers advantages, but these retailers also have large capital investments and limited hours within those physical structures (Enders and Jelassi 2000; White and Daniel 2004). The Internet, on the other hand, has low entry and establishment costs for sellers (Peterson, Balasubramanian, and Bronnenberg 1997). Online retailers are also afforded a wider audience reach, larger product selection, and unlimited operating hours but face a more difficult task in establishing a brand name and developing trust with potential customers (Enders and Jelassi 2000; White and Daniel 2004).

A study by Kaufman-Scarborough and Lindquist (2002) indicated that shoppers differed in their use of channels based on their perceptions of convenience, while others preferred the store setting and rejected other channels. Also suggested, disabled consumers who could not easily purchase at a brick-and-mortar store are good targets for online shopping. Lee and Tan (2003) suggested that retailers should focus on "less risk-averse consumers as their initial target" to help alleviate some of the perceived risks customers may feel in moving into online shopping. Noble, Griffith, and Weinberger (2005) looked at consumer channel utilization across several retail channels, instead of a select few, finding that there were underlying utilitarian values influencing consumer utilization across channels. For example, in adopting the Internet for apparel shopping, prior experience with in-home apparel shopping, as well as the Internet, predicted online apparel buying intention (Yoh et al. 2003). Montoya-Weiss, Voss, and Grewal (2003) suggested customer satisfaction with a service provider is determined by quality across channels, which could influence online channel usage. In addition, Zettelmeyer (2000) argued that firms could use pricing and communication information strategically on multiple channels in order to segment their customers and increase their market power.

Retailers looking at a multichannel strategy enhance the shopping experience for their customers by responding to customers in the channels that would garner the best shopping experience, highlighting the value of each channel and adapting each channel to its abilities (Mathwick,

Malhotra, and Rigdon 2002). For example, bricks and mortar retailers emphasize their physical structures to enhance the tactile shopping experience, whereas e-commerce retailers accentuate information sharing, and m-commerce advantages of location and time specificity, as well as personalization.

Omnichannel Marketing

Consumers do not tie themselves to a specific channel. A consumer does not respond to the terms e-commerce or m-commerce. Consumers shop. Consumers want convenience. This expediency may mean overlapping channels. For example, a customer goes to a store and the particular item needed is not in stock, or at a higher price than the customer expects. Using a smartphone, the customer checks online inventory, compares prices, then purchases while on the phone. This customer is using several marketing channels for a single purchase. This type of shopping is omnichannel shopping as shown in Figure 5.1.

Omnichannel refers to the phenomenon of consumers identifying all retail channels as seamless, meaning an integration of all retail channels whether online or offline. Omnichannel offers a smooth transition from one channel to another to the point consumers do not notice a difference. Consumers interact in more than one marketing channel during a shopping experience. Over 60 percent of consumers use four or more channels

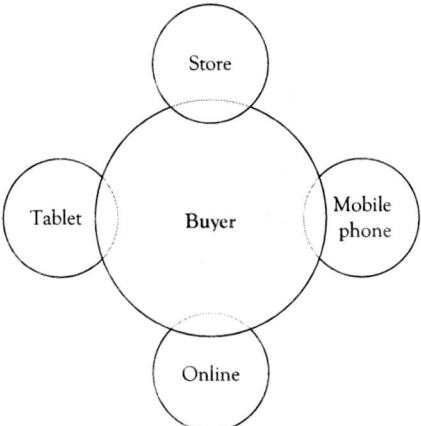

Figure 5.1 Omnichannel shopping experience

per day (Experian Marketing Services 2014). Omnichannel commerce is seamless and moves along with the customer. Omnichannel marketing should be just as fluid. These channels can include, and not limited to, physical stores, websites, kiosks, catalogs, television shopping, social media, and mobile applications. The goal of businesses is to know the target—where the shopping experience will take place.

Integrating the Shopping Experience

Firms must also understand that the total shopping experience is based on the consumer's decision-making process. The experience does not begin when the customer types in the URL, or walks into the store. Many important decisions are made by that point. The shopping experience starts at the point of want or need. Hunger decides on a hamburger. By the time someone walks into McDonald's, the decision has been made. It is important to be a part of the entire decision-making process. The ability of that same person to peruse the menu on the desktop computer, preorder on their smartphone, and pick up at the drive-thru window makes the decision easier because of the expediency within each marketing channel.

Offering consumers the ability to commingle channels gives businesses the opportunity to expand the shopping experience as well as customer retention. Companies that have omnichannel programs achieve a 91 percent higher year-over-year increase in customer retention rate on average. These companies were also able to increase their customer lifetime value 3.4 percent (Cunnane 2013). However, in developing an omnichannel experience, companies must ensure that the channels reflect the preferences of the consumer.

Omnichannel shopping experiences for buyers is seamless, though many companies silo marketing channels. For example, after developing websites, many retailers kept operations between online and offline separate. However, customers did not. Customers would purchase online, and then return a product to the store. Store managers would not accept returned merchandise purchased online. After all, website merchandise and store merchandise were separate. Customers felt that since both carried the same name, online and offline were the same. Customers were left bewildered. There was no separation. If a store and a website had the same name—they were the same company. Many retailers have learned from this experience, now allowing consumers to buy online and pick up at the store.

For retailers, this multichannel approach to shopping comes with its own opportunities and challenges. There are several types of shoppers who are challenging to merchants:

- The research shopper—consumers who research a product in one channel and then purchase in another (Verhoef, Neslin, and Vroomen 2007).
- Free riders—consumers who are more likely to use shopping as a leisure activity (Bloch and Richins 1983) than for specific product information search.
- Browsers—consumers are more likely to use shopping as a leisure activity (Bloch and Richins 1983) than for specific product information search as in showrooming. Browsing allows shoppers the ability to collect information about products that they might be considering to purchase either immediately or in the future (Rowley 2001).
- Showroomers—a form of research shoppers that after an Internet search, evaluates products at the store, and then purchases online or at a competitive store, based on information derived from the store evaluation.

Showrooming refers to the use of the offline by consumers for product research in order to purchase either online or from a competitor at a lower price (Zimmerman 2012).

Big box store retailers, such as Best Buy, find that many consumers use store employees to learn more about products, and then buy them from other retailers online after investigating which products to purchase. Retailers have tried to offset this practice through price matching; however, matching price becomes a short-term fix for a larger problem. Mobile phone use by consumers has led to an increase in showrooming practices. Consumers use their mobile phones to research online pricing, or in the case of retail stockouts, contact other consumers for price and stock information at competing stores.

Showrooming is a challenge. While in the store, 59 percent of smart-phone users checked online for discounts. However, over 90 percent checked a different retailer's site for pricing information (Moth 2014). Retailers need an understanding of the dimensions of showrooming in order to develop marketing strategies that allow for the integration of all channels, while making sure that cannibalization is inhibited.

In each case, whether showrooming, research shopping, free riding, or browsing, retailers provide the costs of services without the benefit of obtaining revenue support (Burns 2010). Companies are now looking at different digital technologies to overcome these costs, and increase the value of the shopping experience for buyers.

Converging Offline, E-Commerce, and M-Commerce on the Path to Purchase

The decision-making process that leads to buying is considered the path to purchase. For many it begins with a want or need, ending with obtain-ing the product or service for fulfillment. To enrich the path to purchase, firms look to technology to boost omnichannel shopping experiences.

Retailers turned to kiosks to link in-store and mobile cross-channel marketing. Kiosks refer to in-store information stands, usually with an installed computer or display screen. There are mall kiosks used for prod-uct display and points of purchase. However, many retailers use these stands in-store for product information, bridal/baby registry informa-tion, and the store directory. By linking kiosks to websites, retailers offer product information and points of purchase, allowing for self-service enhancement and an atmosphere in which the customer is familiar. The problem with these stands is that the customer has to seek it out within the store. A kiosk store directory is useless if the kiosk cannot be located. The other challenge is for businesses in which the use of a kiosk is not justifiable in terms of cost or consumer experience.

Several businesses use in-store tablets to bridge the e-commerce/m-commerce gap. Armed with tablets, sales associates are becoming walking kiosks. "Can I help you" has taken on a whole new meaning as sales associates are able to look up product information, as well as become point-of-sale to check out customers anywhere in the store. Less expensive than conventional registers, tablet-based point of sale systems have increased (Evans 2013) and is convenient for customers. These systems mobilize the sales associates to give information to consumers at the decision point and reduce checkout lines—allowing for quick purchase decision making.

Integration of tablet use by customers on premise allows merchants to integrate the path to purchase into an omnichannel experience. Service merchants, such as hotels, cruise ships, and airlines, can offer concierge services through mobile devices for increased consumer convenience without sacrificing personalized service.

Express check-in/checkout, amenity requests, food orders, dining reservation requests, tour booking functions, and other services can be provided through tablet apps and websites while a consumer is on a business trip or pleasure vacation. Guests can provide trip information prior to a visit, then, according to guests needs, hotels and cruise ships can provide customized programs for each guest, airlines can provide specified meals, and all can provide individualized discounts and deals based on the customers' itinerary to enhance the experience.

Consumer-friendly, easy to browse, and intuitive websites and applications enable the enhancement of the service experience (Evans 2014). Heeding the content is king mantra, the omnichannel experience should allow for ease of use, delighting the customer in every step of the experience. Every part of the experience should be laced with specific calls to action, giving customers routes along their path.

Enlightening the Digital Path to Purchase with Beacons

Most marketing executives agree that customer experience is an area in which companies need to develop. In focusing on customer experience improvement, 33 percent of marketers felt that making the experience personal and relevant was most important; however, 27 percent said this is also where companies need skill development (e-Marketer February 2015).

Firms understand that technology can help bridge the offline, e-commerce, and m-commerce gaps in the omnichannel experience. Using tablet computers, by sales associates and other front-line employees, aids in developing skills as well as the use of mobile technology to improve customer relationships. However, companies must learn those technologies acceptable to customers. Companies must remember—convenience.

The use of QR codes—quick response codes—was thought to bridge offline and online. However, QR codes are not convenient for consumers. QR codes are an offshoot of barcodes. QR codes are readable tags that contain data and are readable through a QR reader. QR codes can be placed in any location—within a store, advertisement, or packaging. QR codes can store website addresses, product information, or any information a consumer would need before purchase. Yet, in order to read the code, consumers must download the QR code reader. There are several steps involved in decoding: Taking a picture of the code, downloading the code into the reader, reading the information, or connecting to the website. Since there are several types of QR codes, consumers need several readers, making the codes inconvenient. Although marketers use QR codes, consumers have not caught on.

Other technologies have come to market to continue in convergence of the omnichannel pathways. Proximity marketing refers to technology that localizes information within a certain area. Through digital tagging, merchants can engage customers at specific locations with marketing promotions that are timely and relevant to the customer. Two types of proximity marketing—near field communications (NFC) and Bluetooth Low Energy (BLE) beacons—are merging offline and mobile for personalized buying experiences.

NFC allows for mobile payments in-store. NFC is a form of communication between two devices, usually a mobile phone, and a contactless payment system, and is used for contactless payments when the consumers' mobile devices are equipped. NFC relies on a chip to link a customer's mobile device with a retailer's technology through electromagnetic radio fields within close proximity. Near field communication can establish a secure environment for transactions using encryption.

NFC can be used also with tags similar to RFID tags. Each works within radio frequency. NFC tags, like QR codes, are embedded into products, signage, and other areas where a customer frequents. Unlike QR codes, no readers are involved. The information is read directly from the consumer's mobile, tablet, or smartphone when the device is in the area of the tag. Retailers can place NFC tags on or near products for extended advertising and information. Special offers, coupons, and discounts can aid in boosting sales through NFC when placed at strategic locations. The challenge of NFC concerns engagement as the devices of consumers must be enabled in a short distance range. In addition, NFC is slower than Bluetooth in terms of speed, but consumes less power.

BLE refers to the use of beacons that constantly transmit information for the exchange of data over distances up to 500 ft. The beacons can be placed anywhere in a mall, airport, store, stadium, restaurant, or any other place of business. The beacons transmit information to consumer devices that are in proximity, and can be battery-powered or have a fixed power source, which means beacons can be placed anywhere. Beacons can be placed in mannequins to give information on clothing. BLE in airport terminals can connect passengers for updated travel information.

Programming beacons allows retailers to send out personalized messages. Consumers can be informed concerning product information, sales, and quick checkout. However, consumers must have their Bluetooth available, turned on, and the information accepted.

Linking physical locations with mobile commerce also links the firm with the customer. Firms can connect with mobile devices in order to inform the consumer while in-store. Is electronic commerce bypassed? No. Beacon technology can track a shopper's movements in the store, gathering information on how the consumer shops. Information concerning this journey enables merchants to understand the shopping experience—data that can be used to increase the consumer's shopping experience both offline and online.

Questions

1. What is the difference between multichannel and omnichannel?
2. Name three consumer touchpoints significant to e-commerce.
3. How can businesses use QR codes effectively for marketing?
4. What is the difference between NFC and BLE?
5. What is proximity marketing?
6. List five different industries and discuss how each can use beacons for business success.

CHAPTER 6

Enhancing Digital Commerce

In discussing the future of shopping, Burke (1997) urged managers to take an active role in defining and managing the future of the Internet. Technology plays an important role in the shopping process and the optimization of technology should be taken into consideration when defining a shopping experience (Burke 2002). Overall, the Internet has heightened the overall shopping experience for both firms and consumers. The Internet allows for anywhere, anytime shopping for consumers. Firms are able to increase their market, granularly define their market, and create deeper relationships with customers as well as supply chain partners.

The interactivity of the Internet is the most compelling argument for online, as it allows the consumer and retailer to communicate one-on-one. Yet, in going online, retailers must also provide consumers with satisfaction with the entire online experience. Online shopping added a new dimension to service for retailers, as it allowed for easier and faster feedback from customers. It also created growing pains with respect to product delivery, privacy, security, and online transactions. E-commerce has been a panacea for firms looking for interactivity with their customers. It has allowed for services such as information content, feedback to and from customers, and most importantly, the development of relationships with customers not found in traditional channels. Digital commerce offers an online experience that allows for relationships that are more individual with customers not seen since the early days of retailing.

The location and time specificity, as well as the personalization advantage of m-commerce allows marketers to use m-commerce as a platform to garner greater customer satisfaction than other marketing channels. Faster response times to customer needs, questions, and inquiries are possible in m-commerce. Firms respond to the specific individual in need of attention, which conveys a sense of privacy and confidentiality.

NFC and BLE increases the ability to interact with customers on individual levels, allows for a better understanding of the customer's shopping experience, and integrates vital information for increase in response to customer needs.

Three Dimensionality

Now retailers can develop websites and applications with three-dimensionality to increase customer satisfaction and shopping entertainment. Virtual reality, a blending of real world and technology, aids in the achievement of these goals. Metaverse retailing and augmented reality (AR) are two different types of virtual reality technologies that can give customers the end goals of purchase satisfaction on a journey that is fun and exciting.

Metaverse retailing refers to a virtual space that is three-dimensional whereby users can interact with the environment and other individuals. The three-dimensionality of metaverse retailing allows for a more robust shopping experience. Based on virtual world technology, a three-dimensional graphic representation of the consumer, or avatar, shops within a virtual reality space. Unlike e-commerce websites, metaverse sites simulate real world retail outlets whereby users move throughout the 3-D site as if moving through the aisles of a brick-and-mortar establishment. Development of metaverse retailing for both online and mobile devices is possible.

Recent technological advances also allow more than one user to shop together. Now, shopping with friends while online provides for more engaging shopping experiences. For example, a bride can try on a wedding dress through the online metaverse. Her mother and bridesmaids can be a part of the experience—all while online and in various locations. The marketing potential of a metaverse lies in the ability to draw consumers through three-dimensional technology. This 3-D technology has many implications for marketers. However, metaverse retailing is expensive. The infrastructure costs, for now, have outweighed the possible competitive advantage for most businesses.

AR is similar as it combines both virtual and real-world environments. AR overlays digital with real-time for a computer-generated environment that mimics a real world setting. Research of AR finds that compared to traditional e-commerce, AR aids in providing more direct product information for consumers (Lu and Smith 2007). Though the tactile quality of shopping is still missing, shoppers are absorbed into a scene that blends reality with animation.

Unlike e-commerce websites, metaverse and AR sites simulate real-world retail outlets with consumers interacting with products, moving through aisles, and choosing products. Instead of reading transaction logs, as is done for online shopping, or even tracking how someone navigates through a site, marketers can now have a visual representation of consumer movements throughout the virtual store. Virtually, marketers can see the experience of shopping as it is happening. Interaction between shoppers, employees, and others can be seen and heard. The information gleaned from a virtual store can be used further to develop either the "brick" or "click" location for businesses.

Is there enough consumer motivation for retailers to invest in virtual reality retailing? In examining rotational visual simulation used to create the 3D experience as product presentation on an e-commerce site, rotation positively influenced perceived information quality, mood, attitude, and purchase intention (Park, Stoel, and Lennon 2008). Virtual reality allows retailers to highlight their wares in a social environment. However, firms need to identify what consumers are looking for in terms of shopping in any reality. Consumers are more likely to shop in these three-dimensional outlets if the sites are useful and convenient. Careful attention should be made in terms of the ease in which consumers can maneuver and navigate through the site—whether it is a website or mobile application. As with any other websites, easy navigation and pertinent content are key to consumer adoption.

Retailers should also consider atmospherics as well as the entertainment value of a virtual reality site. Consumers are looking for enjoyment. Virtual world stores allow retailers to develop the richness of the Internet in a three-dimensional environment. Retailers should take advantage of these resources to attract, maintain, and engage consumers.

In terms of digital commerce, virtual reality mixes offline, e-commerce, and m-commerce. Shopping comes alive. An immersive experience brings the shopping experience to another level for consumers through the three-dimensionality of virtual reality. Moving through the aisles of a physical location, selecting through a large assortment of goods and services as with online, combined with both the social ability and individualization of mobile gives virtual reality a unique blend of marketing qualities to make shopping a unique experience for the consumer.

The Internet of Things

Machine-to-machine communications actually defines the Internet of things (IOT). However, IOT is redefining access to the Internet. Connectivity to the Internet is not limited to communication devices. Tesla cars, for example, will preheat or precool for you depending upon the weather.

For firms, enabling devices to connect to the Internet, IOT allows for real-time information sharing that gives firms the ability to track inventory, enable efficient delivery tracking monitoring, and customize offers as well as delivery option.

Digital commerce will evolve beyond electronic and mobile as home appliances detect consumer needs. Electricity bills can be cut as the clothes dryer alerts you on your television or smartphone when it is about to finish. Lights can turn on and off depending on your schedule. Your trips to the grocery store, or even shopping online, can be lessened as refrigerators and cabinets can connect with grocery stores to place automatic food, pantry, and toiletry orders.

Wearables, however, are the most preferred of the IOT devices to catch the attention of most consumers. Wearables are those devices embedded with software or sensors to connect objects to the Internet in order to exchange data with another connected device. Watches, shoes, shirts, glasses, and headphones are just some of the wearables that are used for IOT purposes.

Watches and wristbands have become the most popular of the wearables in the past few years. Watches are now synced with smartphones to become smartwatches that allow users to receive messages, send texts, play music, and track fitness activities. Wristbands, with connectivity to smartphones, allow the user to track heart rate, walking distance, and other fitness measures.

All of this collected information brings opportunities to marketers for more precision in detecting consumer needs. Understanding how consumers use products. Understanding when to deliver products. Understanding how much and when products are used by specific target markets. IOT will aid in precise marketing—the ability to target precise targets and products to meet precise needs. Precise marketing aids digital commerce beyond both electronic and mobile; however, it will make both e-commerce and m-commerce more efficient for both the marketer and the consumer.

Gamification

Applying the elements of a game in marketing aids in motivating and engaging customers, including competition with others, score keeping, rules of play, and rewarding with points. Gamification refers to the addition of game features to a task to encourage participation (*Merriam-Webster* 2015).

Many firms use gamification in developing loyalty programs. Rewarding a number of purchases with points for future purchases in order to maintain repeat customers is a technique based on gamification. Others reward points based on online contributions including product reviews, uploaded photos and videos with the product, and sharing on Facebook or other social media site. Foursquare used gaming as a service. Customers could become the "mayor" of an establishment with frequent visits.

Digital commerce makes gamification an easy addition to any marketing program. Basing rewards, points, and competitions on those areas that are important to the marketer can lead to better product reviews, more Facebook likes, or product sales. Using gaming apps are ways through which mobile commerce objectives can be achieved. Fun activities on apps are more likely to be used than just filling out forms. Starbucks My Rewards gives consumers the goal of filling a cup with stars to earn a free drink or food. This is much more fun than having a card punched.

Using gamification can reward the firm with loyal customers, purchases that are more frequent, and better reviews. However, gamification must be used with caution.

- Understand your target and their willingness to play
- Use reward systems that lead to customer motivation and engagement
- Make sure the competition in the games is fair
- Deliver the content creatively
- Make the game elements interchangeable for offline, online, and mobile touchpoints

3D Printers

3D printing technology enables users to develop objects, unlike most printers that combine ink and paper. 3D printers replicate objects in three dimensions, building one layer at a time based on computer input. Though 3D printers can produce body parts, housing, and rocket engine parts, developing household products for everyday use is now possible.

There are many advantages to having a 3D printer in the home. There is no need for tools, molds, or other paraphernalia for printing. The printer obtains information from a computer. The extrusion material is an organic polymer, and, with certain printers, using food for the product is possible.

Replacement parts, small household objects, and personal items are just some of the products that someone can print at home. Instead of waiting for a replacement part, consumers can download the assembly instructions from the website and produce the part from their 3D printer.

3D printers can become another customer touchpoint as some companies are making available their products for development in 3D printers. It can change the way of product manufacturing. This can become another way of customizing products. For example, Hershey announced that consumers can make their chocolate bars at home in 3D printers. Chocolate lovers can stream chocolate into their own designs. When given the basic product, consumers can add their own extra ingredients, such as buying basic shampoos, and then adding various aromas to personalize the products. Not only can the manufacturer sell the shampoo but the additives as well.

3D printing is also pushing digital commerce in a new direction. Amazon has an area specifically for 3D products. Customers can buy and sell 3D printed objects including jewelry, toys, electronics, and products for the home. Other companies allow consumers to design 3D products, and sell them on the company website. Shapeways, for example, will allow consumers to upload products, produce them, and sell them based on the customer's designs. This digital commerce business model allows the customer to be manufacturer and consumer.

These trends in the digital marketplace are transforming electronic commerce and mobile commerce. Where this transformation is leading is anyone's guess. However, in each case, the customer's needs must be met. Enhancement of digital commerce still refers to maintaining the expectations of the customer through the 4Ps—the right product, at the right price, promoting to the best target, at the place (or touchpoint) where the target will purchase.

Questions

1. How can metaverse retailing integrate the offline and online shopping experience?
2. Name three ways augmented reality can be used effectively to enhance the shopping experience.
3. How will consumers respond to IOT in the home?
4. Describe how to incorporate gamification into m-commerce.
5. Are 3D printers a threat to retailers?

Conclusions

What Else Matters?

In all of marketing, the customer matters. Knowing the right customer matters more. Understanding how the right customer makes a path through the omnichannel matters most.

Connectivity. Connecting through e-commerce or m-commerce is more than the device. It is about knowing whom you are connecting with, connecting through communication, and understanding your customers' challenges in omnichannel shopping. Connectivity may mean different devices, 3D printers, for example, where the commerce is developed by the customer through means supplied by the company.

Customer. Understanding who the customer is has become harder. E-commerce customers began as those who frequented physical locations. As online changed, the online customers become less local and more global. M-commerce customer targets became more granular—less global, more local. The need for each is different. Time constraints, pricing, and information aid in need identification for the differences in each segment. Understand these differences in order to understand your targets.

Convenience. Close to home, easy to navigate website, free app. Convenience means different things to different targets. Nevertheless, in all cases, the path to purchase should be convenience to every customer. To understand your customer's route, go through the process to understand what your customer experiences. Understand each consumer touchpoint. Move through the e-commerce website, and then download the app. Does the online website make purchasing convenient? Does the app make information easily accessible? Does the online website and the mobile app harmonize the path to purchase?

Communication. How are you talking to your target? Does your customer understand what you are saying? Are you saying what your customers need to hear? Concise, to the point, and clear information is needed by customers when online. Concise, to the point, and clear information is also needed by customers when mobile. Online consumers look to decide between alternatives based on information, including price. Mobile consumers are ready to make the purchase decision and looking for the decision-maker, usually price. Providing the right content can make your product or service the resulting decision.

Challenges. Businesses are still trying to understand how e-commerce and m-commerce fit into the omnichannel shopping experience. The big reveal is that consumers are also trying to find their way through the pathways of offline, online, and mobile. Consumers are looking to business to get it right. Business is looking to consumers for answers. Accepting the fact that all routes are being undertaken, businesses should make each pathway filled with the right customer, know concerns, and make the omnichannel shopping experience a conduit of convenience as we all learn digital commerce integration.

Consolidation. Each touchpoint must reflect the retailer's value to the customer. The omnichannel experience should harmonize so that a consumer, in their mind, sees a retailer as one. Each touchpoint must associate with the next. The retailer, whether online or offline, is consolidated into one entity. Marketers must understand this consolidation by making sure of the connectivity between consumer touchpoints.

Hopefully, the information supplied in this book will enable you to mesh your digital marketing efforts—online, offline, mobile, and social—harmoniously in order to attract, retain, and understand your customers.

Questions

1. What is the best way to integrate the limitlessness of e-commerce with the social or personal qualities m-commerce into the consumer shopping experience?
2. What is the future of digital commerce?

References

Arnott, D.C., and S. Bridgewater. 2002. "Internet, Interaction and Implications for Marketing." *Marketing Intelligence and Planning* 20, no. 2, pp. 86–95.

Bellman, S., R.F. Potter, S. Treleaven-Hassard, J.A. Robinson, and D. Varan. 2011. "The Effectiveness of Branded Mobile Phone Apps." *Journal of Interactive Marketing* 25, no. 4, pp. 191–200.

Biyalogorsky, E., and P. Naik. 2003. "Clicks and Mortar: The Effect of On-Line Activities on Off-Line Sales." *Marketing Letters* 14, no. 1, pp. 21–32.

Bloch, P.H., and M.L. Richins. 1983. "Shopping Without Purchase: An Investigation of Consumer Browsing Behavior." *Advances in Consumer Research* 10, no. 1, pp. 389–93.

Branding Brand. 2015. "Branding Brand Mobile Commerce Index". *White Paper*. http://share.brandingbrand.com/share/data/Branding-Brand_Mobile-Commerce-Index_January-2015.pdf (accessed February 15, 2015).

Brengman, M., M. Geuens, B. Weijters, S.M. Smith, and W.R. Swinyard. 2005. "Segmenting Internet Shoppers Based on Their Web-Usage-Related Lifestyle: A Cross-Cultural Validation." *Journal of Business Research* 58, no. 1, pp. 79–88.

Brohan, M. 2015. "Asia Hits the E-Commerce Fast Track." *Internet Retailer*. https://www.Internetretailer.com/2015/02/10/asia-hits-e-commerce-fast-track (accessed February 15, 2015).

Burke, R. 1997. "Do You See What I See? The Future of Virtual Shopping." *Journal of the Academy of Marketing Science* 25, no. 4, pp. 352–60.

Burke, R. 2002. "Technology and the Customer Interface: What Consumers Want in the Physical and Virtual Store." *Journal of the Academy of Marketing Science* 30, no. 4, pp. 411–32.

Burns, D.J. 2010. "Consumer Alienation and Attitudes Toward Consumer Free Riding." *The Journal of Business* 9, no. 1, pp. 22–36.

Callard, A. May 2014. "Tablets Become a More Popular Shopping Device." *Internet Retailer*. https://www.Internetretailer.com/2014/05/15/tablets-become-more-popular-shopping-device (accessed February 15, 2015).

Chandon, P., V.G. Morwitz, and W.J. Reinartz. 2004. "The Short-and Long-Term Effects of Measuring Intent to Repurchase." *Journal of Consumer Research* 31, no. 3, pp. 566–72.

Clulow, V., C. Barry, and J. Gerstman. 2007. "The Resource-Based View and Value: The Customer-Based View of the Firm." *Journal of European Industrial Training* 31, no. 1, pp. 19–35.

comScore. November 2014. "comScore Forecasts 16 Percent Growth to $61 Billion in 2014 U.S. Holiday E-Commerce Spending on Desktop and Mobile." http://www.comscore.com/Insights/Press-Releases/2014/11/com Score-Forecasts-16-Percent-Growth-to-61-Billion-Dollar-in-2014-US-Holiday-E-Commerce-Spending (accessed February 15, 2015).

Constantinides, E. 2004. "Influencing the Online Consumer's Behavior: The Web Experience." *Internet Research* 14, no. 2, pp. 111–26.

Christensen, C.M., and R.S. Tedlow. 2000. "Patterns of Disruption in Retailing." *Harvard Business Review* 78, no. 1, pp. 42–45.

Criteo. 2014. "State of Mobile Commerce". *White Paper*. http://www.criteo. com/resources/mobile-commerce/ (accessed February 15, 2015).

Cunnane, C. May 2013. "Omni-Channel Retailing 2013." Aberdeen Group. http://www.enterprisemanagement360.com/wp-content/files_mf/139 6617550AberdeenOmniChannelRetailingQuestforHolyGrail.pdf

Doherty, N., F. Ellis-Chadwick, and C. Hart. 2003. "An Analysis of the Factors Affecting the Adoption of the Internet in the UK Retail Sector." *Journal of Business Research* 56, no. 11, pp. 887–97.

Einav, L., J. Levin, I. Popov, and N. Sundaresan. 2014. "Growth, Adoption, and Use of Mobile E-Commerce." *The American Economic Review* 104, no. 5, pp. 489–94.

e-Marketer. 2015. "Mobile Commerce Roundup." e-Marketer. https://www.emarketer.com/public_media/docs/eMarketer_Mobile_Commerce_Roundup.pdf

e-Marketer. February 2015. "Marketers Plan Customer Experience Makeover". e-Marketer. http://www.emarketer.com/Article/Marketers-Plan-Customer-Experience-Makeover/1012015

Enders, A., and T. Jelassi. 2000. "The Converging Business Models of Internet and Bricks-and-Mortar Retailers." *European Journal of Marketing* 18, no. 5, pp. 542–50.

Erdem, S.A., and R.L. Utecht. 2002. "Marketing on the Net: A Critical Review." *Journal of American Academy of Business* 2, no.1, pp. 102–05.

Evans, K. October 2013. "Tablets Are Making Cash Registers a Thing of the Past." *Internet Retailer.* https://www.Internetretailer.com/2013/10/07/tablets-are-making-cash-registers-thing-past (accessed February 15, 2015).

Evans, K. January 2014. "Making the Case for a Great Tablet App." *Internet Retailer.* https://www.internetretailer.com/2014/01/14/making-case-great-tablet-app (accessed October 5, 2015).

Experian Marketing Services. September 2014. "Trending Now: What Savvy Marketers Should Be Doing Right This Minute." *White Paper* http://www.experian.com/assets/marketing-services/white-papers/trending-now.pdf (accessed February 15, 2015).

Fahy, J., and A. Smithee. 1999. "Strategic Marketing and the Resource Based View of the Firm." *Academy of Marketing Science Review* 10, no. 1, pp. 1–21.

Forbes Insights. 2013. "The Connected Executive: Mobilizing the Path to Purchase." *Forbes*, July.

Forsythe, S.M., and B. Shi. 2003. "Consumer Patronage and Risk Perceptions in Internet Shopping." *Journal of Business Research* 56, no. 11, pp. 867–75.

Google Research. 2012. "Mobile-Friendly Sites Turn Visitors to Customers." http://googlemobileads.blogspot.com/2012/09/mobile-friendly-sites-turn-visitors.html (accessed February 15, 2015).

Haas, R. 2002. "The Austrian Country Market: A European Case Study on Marketing Regional Products and Services in a Cyber Mall." *Journal of Business Research* 55, no. 8, pp. 637–46.

Hamill, J. 1997. "The Internet and International Marketing." *International Marketing Review* 14, no. 5, pp. 300–23.

Han, S.P., A. Ghose, and K. Xu. December 2013. "Mobile Commerce in the New Tablet Economy." In *Proceedings of the International Conference on Information Systems (ICIS 2013)*. Milan.

Hoar, A. October 2012. "US B2B eCommerce Sales to Reach $559 Billion by the End of 2013." *Forrester Research.* http://blogs.forrester.com/andy_hoar/12-10-18-us_b2b_ecommerce_sales_to_reach_559_billion_by_the_end_of_2013 (accessed February 15, 2015).

Hritzuk, N., and K. Jones. 2014. *Multiscreen Marketing: The Seven Things You Need to Know to Reach Your Customers Across TVs, Computers, Tablets, and Mobile Phones.* Hoboken, NJ: John Wiley & Sons.

IAB. 2014. "Apps and Mobile Web: Understanding the Two Sides of the Mobile Coin." Internet Advertising Bureau. *White Paper.* http://www.iab.net/media/file/IAB_Apps_and_Mobile_Web_Final.pdf (accessed February 15, 2015).

IBM. 2014. U.S. Retail Cyber Monday Report 2014. IBM. http://www-01.ibm.com/software/marketing-solutions/benchmark-reports/benchmark-2014-cyber-monday.pdf

Jones, P., C. Clarke-Hill, and D. Hillier. 2002. "Retailing in the UK." *Marketing Intelligence and Planning* 20, no. 4, pp. 229.

Kaufman-Scarborough, C., and J.D. Lindquist. 2002. "E-shopping in a Multiple Channel Environment." *Journal of Consumer Marketing* 19, no. 4, pp. 333–50.

Kim, J., E. Suh, and H. Hwang. 2003. "A Model for Evaluating the Effectiveness of CRM Using the Balanced Scorecard." *Journal of Interactive Marketing* 17, no. 2, pp. 5–19.

Kolesar, M.B., and R.W. Galbraith. 2000. "A Services-Marketing Perspective on E-Retailing: Implications for E-Retailers and Directions for Further Research." *Internet Research* 10, no. 5, pp. 42–38.

Kotler, P. Winter 1973–1974. "Atmospherics as a Marketing Tool." *Journal of Retailing* 49, no. 4, pp. 48–65.

Lederer, A.L., D.A. Mirchandani, and K. Sims. 1997. "The Link Between Information Strategy and Electronic Commerce." *Journal of Organizational Computing and Electronic Commerce* 7, no. 1, pp. 17–34.

Lee, K.S., and S.J. Tan. 2003. "E-Retailing Versus Physical Retailing: A Theoretical Model and Empirical Test of Consumer Choice." *Journal of Business Research* 56, no. 11, pp. 877–85.

Li, H., T. Daugherty, and F. Biocca. 2001. "Characteristics of Virtual Experience in Electronic Commerce: A Protocol Analysis." *Journal of Interactive Marketing* 15, no. 3, pp. 13–30.

Lohse, G.L., S. Bellman, and E.J. Johnson. 2000. "Consumer Buying Behavior on the Internet: Findings from Panel Data." *Journal of Interactive Marketing* 14, no. 1, pp. 15–29.

Lu, Y., and S. Smith. 2007. "Augmented Reality E-Commerce Assistant System: Trying While Shopping." In *Human-Computer Interaction. Interaction Platforms and Techniques*, 643–52. Heidelberg: Springer Berlin.

Lundqvist, A., V. Liljander, J. Gummerus, and A. Van Riel. 2013. "The Impact of Storytelling on the Consumer Brand Experience: The Case of a Firm-Originated Story." *Journal of Brand Management* 20, no. 4, pp. 283–97.

Madrigal, A.S. 2014. "Goldman: There Will Be as Much Mobile Commerce in 2018 as E-Commerce in 2013." *The Atlantic.* http://www.theatlantic.com/technology/archive/2014/03/goldman-there-will-be-as-much-mobile-commerce-in-2018-as-br-e-commerce-in-2013/284270/ (accessed February 15, 2015).

Mathwick, C., N.K. Malhotra, and E. Rigdon. 2002. "The Effect of Dynamic Retail Experiences on Experiential Perceptions of Value: An Internet and Catalog Comparison." *Journal of Retailing* 78, no. 1, pp. 51–60.

Menon, S., and B. Kahn. 2002. "Cross-Category Effects of Induced Arousal and Pleasure on the Internet Shopping Experience." *Journal of Retailing* 78, no. 1, pp. 31–40.

Merriam-Webster. 2015. http://www.merriam-webster.com/dictionary/gamification (accessed August 14, 2015).

Montoya-Weiss, M.M., G.B. Voss, and D. Grewal. 2003. "Determinants of Online Channel Use and Overall Satisfaction with a Relational, Multichannel Service Provider." *Journal of the Academy of Marketing Science* 31, no. 4, pp. 448–58.

Moth, D. January 2014. "50+ Fascinating Stats About Mobile Commerce in the US." *Econsultancy.* https://econsultancy.com/blog/64166-50-fascinating-stats-about-mobile-commerce-in-the-us (accessed February 15, 2015).

Noble, S.M., D.A. Griffith, and M.G. Weinberger. 2005. "Consumer Derived Utilitarian Value and Channel Utilization in a Multi-channel Retail Context." *Journal of Business Research* 58, no. 12, pp. 1643–51.

Novak, T.P., D.L. Hoffman, and Y. Yung. 2000. "Measuring the Customer Experience in Online Environments: A Structural Modeling Approach." *Marketing Science* 19, no. 1, pp. 22–42.

Park, C., and J. Jun. 2003. "A Cross-Cultural Comparison of Internet Buying Behavior: Effects of Internet Usage, Perceived Risks, and Innovativeness." *International Marketing Review* 20, no. 5, pp. 534–53.

Park, J., L. Stoel, and S.J. Lennon. 2008. "Cognitive, Affective and Conative Responses to Visual Simulation: The Effects of Rotation in Online Product Presentation." *Journal of Consumer Behaviour* 7, no. 1, pp. 72–87.

Peterson, R.A., S. Balasubramanian, and B.J. Bronnenberg. 1997. "Exploring the Implications of the Internet for Consumer Marketing." *Journal of the Academy of Marketing Science* 25, no. 4, pp. 329–46.

Pew Research Center. 2013. "In-Store Mobile Commerce During the 2012 Holiday Shopping Season." Pew Internet. http://www.pewInternet.org/files/old-media/Files/Reports/2013/PIP_In_store_mobile_commerce_PDF.pdf (accessed February 15, 2015).

Pew Research Center. 2014. "Mobile Technology Fact Sheet." Pew Internet. http://www.pewInternet.org/fact-sheets/mobile-technology-fact-sheet/ (accessed February 15, 2015).

Phau, I., and S.M. Poon. 2000. "Factors Inflencing the Types of Products and Services Purchased Over the Internet." *Internet Research* 10, no. 2, pp. 102–13.

Reibstein, D.J. 2002. "What Attracts Customers to Online Stores, and What Keeps Them Coming Back?" *Journal of the Academy of Marketing Science* 30, no. 4, pp. 465–73.

Rigby, D. December 2011. "The Future of Shopping." *Harvard Business Review* 89, no. 12, pp. 65–76.

Rowley, J. 2001. "Remodelling Marketing Communications in an Internet Environment." *Internet Research* 11, no. 3, pp. 203–12.

SalesForce. 2014. 2014 Mobile Behavior Report. ExactTarget. http://www.exacttarget.com/sites/exacttarget/files/deliverables/etmc-2014mobilebehaviorreport.pdf (accessed February 15, 2015).

Schoenbachler, D.D., and G.L. Gordon. 2002. "Trust and Consumer Willingness to Provide Information in a Database-Driven Relationship Marketing." *Journal of Interactive Marketing* 16, no. 3, pp. 2–6.

Srivastava, R.K., L. Fahey, and H.K. Christensen. 2001. "The Resource-Based View and Marketing: The Role of Market-Based Assets in Gaining Competitive Advantage." *Journal of Management* 27, no. 6, pp. 777–802.

Swilley, E., and C.F. Hofacker. 2006. "Defining Mobile Commerce in a Marketing Context." *International Journal of Mobile Marketing* 1, no. 2, pp. 18–23.

Verhoef, P.C., S.A. Neslin, and B. Vroomen. 2007. "Multichannel Customer Management: Understanding the Research-Shopper Phenomenon." *International Journal of Research in Marketing*, 24 no. 2, pp. 129–48.

Vrechopoulos, A.P., R.M. O'Keefe, G.I. Doukidis, and G.J. Siomkos. 2004. "Virtual Store Layout: An Experimental Comparison in the Context of Grocery Retail." *Journal of Retailing* 80, no. 1, pp. 13–22.

Wallace, D.W., J.L. Giese, and J.L. Johnson. 2004. "Customer Retailer Loyalty in the Context of Multiple Channel Strategies." *Journal of Retailing* 80, no. 4, pp. 249–63.

White, H., and E. Daniel. 2004. "The Future of On-Line Retailing in the UK: Learning from Experience." *Marketing Intelligence and Planning* 22, no. 1, pp. 10–23.

Wigand, R.T. 1997. "Electronic Commerce: Definition, Theory, and Context." *The Information Society* 13, no. 1, pp. 1–16.

Wikström, S., C. Carlell, and M. Frostling-Henningsson. 2002. "From Real World to Mirror World Representation." *Journal of Business Research* 55, no. 8, pp. 647–54.

Wolfinbarger, M., and M.C. Gilly. 2003. "eTailQ: Dimensionalizing, Measuring and Predicting eTail Quality." *Journal of Retailing* 79, no. 3, pp. 183–98.

Yoh, E., M.L. Damhorst, S. Sapp, and R. Laczniak. 2003. "Consumer Adoption of the Internet: The Case of Apparel Shopping." *Psychology and Marketing* 20, no. 12, pp. 1095–118.

Yuan, L. 2006. "New Domain Name–.Mobi–Could Spur Wireless Web." *The Wall Street Journal*, May 23. New York. http://online.wsj.com/article/SB114834861767160235.html?mod=todays_us_marketplace

Zettelmeyer, F. 2000. "Expanding to the Internet: Pricing and Communications Strategies When Firms Compete on Multiple Channels." *Journal of Marketing Research* 37, no. 3, pp. 292–308.

Zhang, J., and Y. Yuan. 2002. "M-Commerce Versus Internet-Based E-Commerce: The Key Differences." *AMCIS 2002 Proceedings*, pp. 261. Dallas, TX.

Zhuang, Y., and A.L. Lederer. 2006. "A Resource-Based View of Electronic Commerce." *Information and Management* 43, no. 2, pp. 251–61.

Zimmerman, A. 2012. "Showdown Over 'Showrooming.'" *Target*. http://www.wsj.com/articles/SB10001424052970204624204577177242516227440

Index

Virtual reality, 54
Virtual transactions, 1–2
Voss, G.B., 44

Watches and wristbands, 56
Website, 34–35
  atmospherics, 28
  challenges, 27–28
  quality and satisfaction, 28
  small screens, 27

usability and interactivity, 26
Weinberger, M.G., 44
Wi-Fi coverage, 39
Wireless networks, 5

YouTube, 41
Yung, Y., 28

Zettelmeyer (2000), 44

OTHER TITLES IN DIGITAL AND SOCIAL MEDIA MARKETING AND ADVERTISING COLLECTION

Victoria L. Crittenden, Babson College, Editor

- *Viral Marketing and Social Networks* by Maria Petrescu
- *Herding Cats: A Strategic Approach to Social Media Marketing* by Andrew Rohm and Michael Weiss
- *Social Roots: Why Social Innovations Are Creating the Influence Economy* by Cindy Gordon, John P. Girard, and Andrew Weir
- *Social Media Branding For Small Business: The 5-Sources Model* by Robert Davis
- *A Beginner's Guide to Mobile Marketing* by Karen Mishra and Molly Garris
- *Social Content Marketing for Entrepreneurs* by James M. Barry
- *Digital Privacy in the Marketplace: Perspectives on the Information Exchange* by George Milne
- *This Note's For You: Popular Music + Advertising = Marketing Excellence* by David Allan
- *Digital Marketing Management: A Handbook for the Current (or Future) CEO* by Debra Zahay
- *Corporate Branding in Facebook Fan Pages: Ideas for Improving Your Brand Value* by Eliane Pereira Zamith Brito, Maria Carolina Zanette, Benjamin Rosenthal, Carla Caires Abdalla, and Mateus Ferreira
- *Presentation Skills: Educate, Inspire and Engage Your Audience* by Michael Weiss
- *The Connected Consumer* by Dinesh Kumar

Announcing the Business Expert Press Digital Library

Concise e-books business students need for classroom and research

This book can also be purchased in an e-book collection by your library as

- a one-time purchase,
- that is owned forever,
- allows for simultaneous readers,
- has no restrictions on printing, and
- can be downloaded as PDFs from within the library community.

Our digital library collections are a great solution to beat the rising cost of textbooks. E-books can be loaded into their course management systems or onto students' e-book readers.
The **Business Expert Press** digital libraries are very affordable, with no obligation to buy in future years. For more information, please visit **www.businessexpertpress.com/librarians**. To set up a trial in the United States, please email **sales@businessexpertpress.com**.

CPSIA information can be obtained
at www.ICGtesting.com
Printed in the USA
FFOW02n1243250118
44750060-44804FF